GROWTH IN CHRISTIAN FAITH

STRUGGLES, GLIMPSES OF GRACE, LIFE AND FULFILLMENT

For Ben
with best wishes

Leonard

LEONARD DOOHAN

REFLECTIONS ON CONTEMPORARY SPIRITUALITY FOR CHRISTIAN ADULTS (Vol. 3)

The Author

Dr. Leonard Doohan is Professor Emeritus at Gonzaga University, Spokane. He has written 28 books and many articles and has given hundreds of workshops throughout the USA, Canada, Europe, Australia, New Zealand, and the Far East. Doohan's recent books include *Spiritual Leadership: the Quest for Integrity* (2007), *Enjoying Retirement: Living Life to the Fullest* (2010), *Courageous Hope: The Call of Leadership* (2011), *The One Thing Necessary: The Transforming Power of Christian Love* (2012), *Spiritual Leadership: How to Become a Great Spiritual Leader—Ten Steps and a Hundred Suggestions* (2014), *Ten Strategies to Nurture Our Spiritual Lives (2014), Rediscovering Jesus' Priorities (2014),* and *Meditations on Leadership (2017).* Doohan has also written 6 books and given courses and workshops all over the world on the spirituality of John of the Cross (see the list at the end of this book).

Visit leonarddoohan.com

Table of Contents

Preface

This short book deals with some of the many concerns and challenges that people have today regarding their life of faith. There are three parts to the book. In Part I, the book considers some of the many struggles that people must overcome in order to continue as people of faith. Nowadays, it is hard to believe and certainly difficult to distinguish between authentic faith and the clutter of secondary beliefs that confuse and can misdirect people's dedication and enthusiasm. So many believers put their energy into issues that were not primary concerns for Jesus. It is no use denying the problems we face in our society and churches. Rather, we must struggle to grow in faith in spite of the difficulties all around us—whether the growing irrelevance of religion, the worrying trends of social movements that simply use religious language for their political and social goals, or the politicizing of religion. We will have to purify and correct these developments if faith is to survive. In Part II we consider the fact that if faith is to grow we will need to search for reasons to believe, consciously identifying those experiences that we see as glimpses of grace that strengthen faith. We often find that life is full of small things that we are convinced matter intensely, and passionately, and convincingly. These experiences give us hope and when shared in community strengthen our dedication, illumine our faith, and deepen our love in God's self-communication. In Part III we find that in re-committing ourselves to the life that results from faith we nurture that life and discover that God in whom we believe draws us to a greater share in divine life. God does this through our spiritual growth, deeper prayer, participation in the life of the Church, enriching energies of the soul, and deeper union with the Son, our Lord Jesus Christ. So, Part I faces the struggles that challenge our faith, Part II encourages us to keep focused on convincing reasons for faith, and Part III insists we can find life and fulfillment in our dedication to God. Many of the struggles, challenges, and opportunities for re-dedication that I reflect on here can be applied to the various Christian churches, and even other religions, but my primary focus is on the opportunities for growth in faith within the Roman Catholic tradition. The book focuses on adults whose dedication has been weakened or even damaged by failures in contemporary religion.

I would like to suggest to readers that they approach the book in three different tempos. Part I needs courage to face up to the information that comes to us almost on a daily basis and that presents us with struggles we must face in our commitment to faith. We cannot ignore them or neglect to deal with these issues. Let us confront them maturely and ask what they mean for our faith. Part II calls us to open our hearts to see things that maybe we have not seen before and to look at things in ways we have never looked at them before. This will take more reflection than Part I as we carefully seek and discern reasons for our faith in a loving God. Part III challenges us to rededicate ourselves to aspects of our spiritual lives that reveal God to us. This part will require serious thought and meditation, and it will include struggles. As we reflect on several major components of our faith we can examine the depth of our commitment and where necessary renew our self-gift to God. In this very dedication we experience God guiding us.

Part I

STRUGGLING WITH THE CHALLENGES OF FAITH

IT IS GETTING HARDER AND HARDER TO BELIEVE

I am a Roman Catholic and have been all my life. The Church has nurtured and strengthened my faith in God and my knowledge of God's ways, calls, and challenges. In recent decades I have found that the Church focuses too much on itself and on issues that are not central to faith. It seems at times that the Church has assembled a belief system that is no longer centered on Jesus' priorities. There is now a chasm between what I see as authentic faith and the organizational Church's daily agendas. This has led lots of people to a decreased enthusiasm for the Church and for the things of God. For many the Church is now less a light and guide to faith and more of a block hiding God. There is so much uncertainty and problems with human existence in this world and with the Church's inability to lead the way, that unbelief is now a real response for many. Belief in the Church's ability to lead us to God has diminished or even gone for many dedicated Christians, and we are left with lives filled with doubt punctuated by faith. We must remind ourselves that while we may feel upset and confused, confusion can be good for it can challenge us to rethink the core values of our commitment. In these times it is important to know how and what to doubt, how and what to believe.

I have encountered so many people who in spite of the lack of enthusiasm for organized religion are filled with a serious and profound yearning for God and a deep awareness of a realm of life beyond this one. Each of us can ask what are our major beliefs and what is the source of our enthusiasm for faith. Likewise we can ask ourselves which of the Church's current emphases have no interest or importance for us. Certainly, religion in general and Christianity in particular have many enthusiasts, some even fanatical, who pursue ideas, practices, convictions, and agendas that I find are unconnected with faith in God as revealed in Jesus. Much churchgoing does not bring one closer to God but offers comfort in one's chosen values and, at times, justification for one's blindness and biases. At times it seems religion offers us a God whose challenges look like the projects of an NGO. We are left saddened by an image of God who is hidden, asleep, and disinterested. It is harder to believe than it used to be, but we must have the courage to face our doubts and the struggles and failures of religion and have the courage of our convictions about the centrality of faith in God. We can easily hide from the negative experiences of the Church and try to suppress our troubles. But we must face up to our problems. Faith is always about seeing what others do not see. Because we find something difficult to believe does not mean it is unbelievable. All these questions put faith in jeopardy.

In this first part of the book we will look at some of the struggles and challenges to faith. We ask ourselves why are we confused. What is making us struggle to find our faith experience, our spiritual connection and response to Jesus? Nowadays, we often have a sense that something is missing in our spiritual lives within the organizational Church. So, we will consider the confusion that often exists between the three concepts of faith, belief, and religion. We will look at the problem of the increasing irrelevance of religion and religious leaders. We will face up to the worrying trends of social movements substituting for faith. We must ask honestly whether the Church cares about what people of faith care about, and we will ask whether we can accept the pain and darkness of our journey to God. In this first part we ask what are people really saying and thinking. We have to address these concerns; we cannot ignore the illness, the causes of our depression, the symptoms and reasons for the decline of faith

In part two of the book we will search for reasons to deepen our faith, and in part three seek renewal of life and fulfillment in God.

Chapter One
FAITH, BELIEF, AND RELIGION

Faith

"When the Son of Man comes, will he find faith" (Lk 18:8)

The evangelist Luke tells us about a great journey that Jesus made from Galilee to Jerusalem during which he gave a series of important teachings to his disciples. In these critical insights into discipleship, Jesus tells the story of a judge who was not motivated by values or integrity but by the selfish desire to get rid of a woman who kept insisting on gaining justice. Jesus concludes the story by addressing his disciples with a question filled with sadness. "When the Son of Man comes, will he find faith on earth?" (Lk 18:8). The judge was not motivated by justice or faith or values or spiritual convictions, but by selfishness. If Jesus were to return to earth in our times he would find lots of belief systems and plenty of religion, but would he find any faith? *Our generation suffers from a profound loss of a sense of faith.* Jesus was sad that the judge's life was not motivated by faith in a vision of God. So many people today, including many who think of themselves as Christians, live like the judge. They do not do things because they are motivated by faith but for convenience, power, money, and other corrupting values. At times, their religion and even belief systems are unconnected with faith. Like the judge, their responses must include a change in how they treat other people.

Faith is a way of life that results from awareness of God's transforming love in our lives. It includes a challenge to live differently because of this awareness of God's love, and it is based on a conviction that this knowledge of God is revealed to us in Jesus Christ. The idea that God loves humanity and calls men and women to a deep and intimate relationship is beyond our normal categories of understanding. We only know of this because of the revelations of Jesus Christ, the incarnation or embodiment of God's love for us. So, faith is a particular approach to life, personal existence, and destiny because of our acknowledgment of God's love for us.

Faith leads to conversion. This awareness leads to a new way of living, a spirituality, an ongoing conversion in our relationship with God and with others in the human community. It is an intimate awareness and knowledge of God that leads us to trusting surrender, obedience, commitment, and a desire for encounter. It is not something we earn but a gift of God; we become aware that God has taken hold of us and endows us with divine presence, power, and intimacy. So, faith is a gift of power to live differently because of God's grace. When we experience, or become aware of, God's love in Christ, we cannot do anything else except respond with total surrender to God's love and give ourselves to a new way of living because of this love.

Faith is not merely an intellectual assent to truths; it is not that we take hold of a set of values and make them our own, but rather that we realize and accept that God has taken hold of us and made us God's own. The judge did not appreciate that, and neither do many contemporary Christians in business, politics, healthcare, military, and organized religion. They mouth religious statements but they lack the depth of faith.

Faith is a way of knowing God and the life God wants for us— glimpses from time to time. No one knows God by accumulating knowledge, information, and intellectual insight, including that which comes from a religious organization like the Church—even though these community articulations help. Only by abandoning whatever knowledge we previously had and sometimes journeying in darkness and unknowing, do we let God become our teacher and guide. We know God more through faith than we do through the accumulation of knowledge. We can earn the latter through our own achievements, but not the former—that is a complete gift from God. Faith is an inner knowledge, experience and communication that produces a life-giving vision of God, a different kind of knowledge based on emptying ourselves of what we think and believe and being filled with God's new self-revelation. This then leads us to change our lives and to focus them on God and on others.

Faith is a grace, an unearned gift from God that calls for a commitment that touches the depths of our being and personality. Responses vary in intensity; some people's faith will be stronger than others—gradual and progressive. Even when permanent, it is always capable of increase or of threat from sin and a life that is contrary to the values of faith. Disciples have made a commitment in faith, but that gift of God needs to grow. The fundamental redirection of our lives to God by faith in Jesus is only the beginning of an ongoing life of faith with its ups and downs. Partial faith does not mean unbelief, but a commitment which has not reached its full potential.

Living in faith means letting go of control over our own lives. When we believe in God, we know we are not in control. Faith is the life of receptivity and gift, and we can feel helpless, drifting a while without seeing the goal. But in the life of faith we are not moving ourselves towards a goal, but being drawn by a loving God towards our goal. Our task is to make sure we do not place any obstacles in the way of the growth God has ordained for us. So many Christians become skilled at creating obstacles to God's interventions in their lives. Faith is a gift of God that enables us to understand our place is this world in light of God's love for us. Faith is a way of looking at reality, at the big picture of God's involvement in our lives and in our world. In fact, faith is a way of life that restructures reality. Faith means commitment, a new relationship of trust—always acting in light of God's will for us in this world. That is what the judge should have done and did not. For each of us faith gives security; it is reliable, it is an answer to human search and yearnings.

Three important concepts

"For man believes with his heart and so is justified"
(Rom 10:10)

Faith that consists in acknowledging and experiencing God's love and building a life centered on a relationship with God is ever more difficult in a secular world that has explanations for everything without God. In such a world God becomes a "deus ex macina" that explains away the meaninglessness of life. *Often the three concepts—faith, belief, and religion become confused* and this leads to a drift away from authentic faith. This happens when people start with religion or religious belonging, identify a belief system contained in the religion, and then try to develop faith in those beliefs. Beliefs can then mislead and take over faith, and we can then get an emphasis on the culture of the Church rather than the Gospel. It is also problematic when a religion makes the organization the main focus of a belief system. Rather, as we have seen, faith starts with an experience or awareness—our own or someone else's—that we accept as giving meaning to our lives. In fact, we feel it defines us and we have faith that this is who we are called to be. Then following on this new awareness of reality we try to articulate this experience to ourselves or to others, and this gives rise to a belief system. We may then decide with like-minded others to institutionalize this belief system in an organized form in religion or accept our place in a religion like Christianity that has already done this.

Religious institutions express in beliefs what faith should mean. They help us find meaning in life with others in community of like mind and desire of a God-directed life. They Thus, they challenge us to ongoing conversion. They are based on the conviction that God has communicated not just to us personally but to the world and explained what men and women ought to do and how they ought to live. Religions generally base their teachings on revelation contained in books, Christianity is distinct in so far as it bases its revelation primarily on a person—Jesus Christ. It is not centered on a series of articles of belief but on developing a relationship of loving commitment with Jesus Christ. So, what arouses faith? Jesus is the ground of faith and the catalyst that leads to faith. Thus, faith is an experience that motivates us in all we do, belief is an articulation, and religion is an institutionalization.

We can have a belief system and no faith. We can go to Church regularly and have no basic experience of God or of transcendent values, or of something that motivates us in everything we do. Contemporary society has plenty of belief systems and lots of religion but often very little faith. Participants in all kinds of religious traditions take the organization's belief systems unquestioningly and confuse beliefs with faith. *Many people's lives are often not based on faith but on belief systems.* Faith must be based on a profound religious experience and not simply an intellectual assent to a series of beliefs. Plenty of people go to Christian churches and their lives give no evidence of faith. Religion can take over from God and become a separate department of life, separated from real life and others' struggles and sufferings. Religion's devotees can get caught up in secondary issues leading to the declining of religion over time and its need of reform. Paul gives us a good tool to measure the authenticity of our religion; commitments are justified when they come from a heart that is transformed in God's love.

In fact, we have arrived at a situation where some belief systems are contrary to faith. Some Christians and especially Christian ministers sprinkle faithless lives with assorted quotes from the Bible, like salt and pepper, and try to persuade us that this religious talk is equivalent to faith. They focus on irrelevancies while leaving the revelation and call of God untouched. Sometimes church-going Christians cannot actually articulate what they believe in and could not persuade others of their relevance. Rather, we must start with an experience or awareness of God's love and presence to us. This is an experience that then motivates us in everything we do—at least we want it to and succeed most of the time. *We express this faith in beliefs and not the other way around.* The common components of these beliefs can be expressed in religious traditions that can help clarify faith and focus on what is central to our surrender and loving self-gift to God.

The Church's role is to pass on and interpret Jesus' teachings under the guidance of the Holy Spirit. So, *official Church teachings should be conscious expressions of the beliefs of the faithful* that are rooted in Jesus' teachings and articulated over time. These formulations can be very helpful but do not replace faith. They are transitory and will need to be reformulated in changing times. Some expressions of beliefs endure and others do not. Thus, some early formulations of Christology and Mariology were replaced with different ones, ministry is understood differently today than it used to be, the political centrality of the Church is no longer viewed as it used to be, the collegiality of bishops is explained differently than in former centuries, and so on.

When we place religion or beliefs first then faith can become weak and irrelevant. Thus, we often have to listen to ministers preaching beliefs that are not central to faith. This becomes especially problematic when believers are uncritical, unthinking, and blindly accept a minister's views. Moreover, arrogant ministers sometimes identify their own often uninformed views with truth and force their belief systems on unfortunate followers. People who go to the various churches can find that they have to listen to sermons on topics secondary to faith while essential matters go unmentioned. Thus, they find no religious nourishment in attending Church and leave. What should be the good news of the Gospel, presented with joy to the community of faith, is replaced with ideas, practices, and social agendas that are not central to the Gospel. Some beliefs are official and others just local. Religions often get cluttered with secondary, non-essential beliefs, some harmless, others detrimental to faith. Of course, some preachers will present self-serving secondary beliefs as essential as we currently see in religions all over the world. In the context of some religions' deteriorating beliefs, one writer voices the question that many confront; "Would you be better off without religion" (Reza Aslan).

Theology

"Always be prepared to make . . . account for the hope that is in you" (1 Pet 3:15)

When we talk about faith we do so with the aid of theology. When we reflect on our experience of God's love for humanity and deepen our awareness of our need for trusting surrender, we find it essential to express all this to others, and to some extent even to ourselves—we need theology to interpret our own faith. We seek to understand more profoundly this mystery that must change the way we live in this world. Our faith seeks understanding and appropriate expressions in belief, even though words alone can never communicate our experiences of God. Belief is a static expression at a given moment in time, whereas theology is an ongoing process.

Theology is a dialogue between the awareness and experience of faith and contemporary culture, and it can help us give meaning to beliefs in changing times and cultures. *Theology is a way of expressing to others something about the profound experiences of faith.* Saint Peter in his first letter told his followers that they should always be ready to give an account of the hope that lies within them. The hope that lies within us comes from faith, and the account is done by means of theology. So, theology is faithfulness to the values and vision of our faith in conversation with others in a community of shared faith and beliefs. As that conversation shifts, so too will beliefs, and they must do so to be faithful to core values in changing times.

Theology means words about God, reflections about God. So for all of us doing theology means making sense out of life, making sense out of relationships, making sense out of our purpose in life, making sense of God's involvement in our lives and world. *Theology is a way of conveying to others why we must live in the way we do.* Perhaps the shortest definition of theology is that it is an interruption. We interrupt daily life and events to bring a different interpretation to them in light of the experience and awareness of the saving power or God. Theology means seeing what other people do not see, and looking at things in ways that others do not—all because of our knowledge of God's interventions in our lives.

Theology helps us pass on our faith to others and invite them to become aware of the power of God in their lives. It helps a community of faith-filled people articulate its shared faith, find appropriate ways of expressing it, and clarify what is, and what is not, central to faith. There must be a balance between change and continuity. At the same time, we discover that people express their experiences of encounter with God in different ways and this calls us to respect and appreciate theological pluralism as part of a community's faith. We also appreciate the intensity of peoples' faith and over time a hierarchy of their beliefs.

A new perspective on life and faith

"He who says he is in the light and hates his brother is in the
darkness still" (1 Jn 2:9)

Theology used to be exclusively deductive; we applied Scripture and Church teachings to daily events. We lived our faith in light of these sources of revelation and teachings. *Nowadays, we take a new perspective on life and faith, beginning with people and their struggles.* So, now it is common to start with a person in a concrete situation, for this is where the challenge to faith now comes. So, we think of the poor and their experience in liberation theology, women and their experiences in feminist theology, blacks in black theology, and so on. For us nowadays, in addition to revealed sources of teachings we also start with our openness and readiness to respond to people in their own situations in life. Theology in each of these contexts is the key; it helps us understand what it means to be fully human and fully Christian. Thus, it helps us become aware of who we are and who we want to become, and what are our relationships and obligations to others, especially those who suffer.

Faith calls for a new relationship with God and a new relationship with others because of our faith in God. We interrupt the situation to bring new light to bear, to see things in a new way—in light of the profound faith experience of God. This experience changes us from selfish to selfless, it makes us live differently. Thinking about other people in their sufferings can be a dangerous memory for it will never allow us to live as we did in the past.

The Church's role in faith development includes presenting its beliefs as means to understand faith and make it ever relevant to changing times. It can be a standard of faith that in our modern world frequently comes under attack. It cannot substitute itself for faith, but must become a beacon of faithfulness. It uses theology to express the meaning of faith in changing times and cultures.

Theology is thus action oriented but based on reflection—we act in light of our experience of God but also in light of our awareness and knowledge of others and their situations in life. Faith leads to a change of life, an ongoing conversion. If all we see is "merely believed-in religion" (J. B. Metz) then religion and beliefs are in decline and there may be no faith. *Faith needs affirmation and confirmation in actions based on our awareness and experience of God's love.* It is frightening to see the disconnect in the United States, and of course in other countries, of people's claimed faith and their political and social views, including oppression, racism, denial of voter rights, inequality, and so on. The first letter of John tells it like it is! Anyone who claims to be in the light of faith but hates his brother or sister is still living in the darkness of unbelief and no faith. Faith must lead us to transform not only ourselves but the situations we experience in daily life.

As we all take responsibility for our growth in faith, we need to keep clearly in mind the important distinctions between faith, beliefs, and religion. This will help give us energy, passion, and dedication for faith while appreciating the appropriate importance to beliefs and religion. It is faith we seek to grow and mature with God's help. Faith and spiritual encounter are fundamental, and they can be supported by beliefs and structures provided the latter are connected to faith.

Personal reflection

I am shocked and saddened when I see how so many religious "leaders" focus their preaching on secondary issues of belief systems in general or local trigger issues that arouse the faithful. Even "faithful" is an unusual term to describe people who rarely focus on faith but immerse themselves in very secondary issues of increasingly irrelevant packaged belief systems. Faith ought to be related to a personal relationship with the living God.

Questions for discussion or personal reflection

1. Does your Christian life center on faith in Jesus or on the beliefs of organized religion? Both are necessary, but how should they be connected?

2. Describe the most important spiritual experience of your life. How does it affect your life daily?

3. How do you interrupt the values of society and present the values of Christ and faith?

Chapter Two

THE GROWING
IRRELEVANCE OF RELIGION
AND RELIGIOUS LEADERS

Religious institutions without spirituality

> *"Because of the increase of evil the love of most will grow cold" (Mt 24:12)*

The years immediately after the second Vatican Council were times of excitement and attractive religious renewal. The Church reminded people of their essential beliefs and involved them in rediscovering the life-giving values that brought them together in a Christ-centered community. In many cases the Church took the lead through a world-wide renewal in reminding people of good will and hope of the vision of faith of which the Church was standard-bearer. The Council focused on people's renewal in a Church seen as a community (not just a hierarchical institution), in the heart of the world (not separated in ascetical isolation), in order to serve the world (not to be served). All kinds of spiritual movements sprung up to promote awareness of the central beliefs of the Catholic Church and to focus and strengthen faith. Pope, bishops, clergy and religious played key roles in uplifting leadership and inspiring commitment, and many of them became saintly models of a pilgrim Church. Those of us who lived through those years remember the enthusiasm and dedication. The Council and through it our faith and beliefs became the central focus of our lives. We gave lots of time and energy, worked together in service with new friends in faith, and saw the importance of a life-giving Church on the entire world and wanted to be a part of it. We acknowledged then as we continue to do now that many friends struggled with the changes of those years. Younger people today who never experienced the thrill of those years cannot understand what they missed or the sadness we now feel in a *Church that has lost its excitement and is no longer what it used to be.* Many believers are now indignant at a Church that appears irrelevant.

A careful reading of the history and daily discussions of the Council show the reluctance of many bishops for the proposed changes and many of them were carried along with the general euphoria that permeated conciliar debate. Within a few years after the closure of the Council, bishops who had challenged their faithful to dedicate themselves to the new teachings were among the first to fall by the wayside. *Some of these leaders stunted the renewal,* and found all kinds of excuses for going back to the way things used to be. They readily attracted many uncommitted church-goers and soon the renewal presented by the Council slowed down. We have now ended with an institution unaware of the conversion and renewal of the Council years and of the decades that followed.

Nowadays the Church is again primarily a hierarchical institution with little impact on the world and its corrupt values, and with little sense of service in its frequently visionless and pompous *leaders who model their administration of Church matters on the corporate world*, and never abdicate their acquired power. In the Sermon on the Mount, Jesus expressed hope that the Church would be the salt of the earth and the light of the world (Mt 5:13-14). In the years of the Second Vatican Council and the years that followed it was, but this is no longer the case. Clearly, there are pockets of ecclesial dedication all over the world and enthusiastic commitment in many local groups. In fact, there are so many wonderful believers, but their enthusiasm is often left un-channeled. However, there is no large-scale spiritual development such as we have seen at other times in the Church's history.

For many Catholics today *there is no enthusiasm in the Church, no important renewal programs for the faithful*, and people do not belong to the Church, they attend it. Clergy are not the great spiritual leaders of former times and religious are few, in fact a dying group. Large numbers of people in the Church love Pope Francis but very few bishops and less curial cardinals have responded to his call for renewal. Local leaders simply offer an ecclesiastical management of spirituality often without commitment and spiritual energy. Church services, with their return to old-fashioned and unintelligible language and rituals, often look like weekly activities in a retirement home. The organization of the Church is now failing us and in doing so it has lost the allegiance of followers. Many Catholics who were in the forefront of renewal after the Council are now suspicious and unreceptive of the Church, lack trust in the direction of the Church, and see no purpose in being involved when Church leaders show such little vision and commitment to renewal. The

Church has more problems today than it has had in most current people's lifetime, and this situation threatens people's faith.

Failed leadership

> *"By your words you will be justified and by your words you*
> *will be condemned" (Mt 12:37)*

The growing irrelevance of the Church to increasing numbers of the faithful is largely due to poor leadership. It is disheartening to look at our Church leaders and depressing to look to the future that our current leaders are likely to produce. We remember great priestly visionary leaders in our communities, men respected by everyone. But for the most part they are gone, replaced by anyone the bishop can find to fill slots in personnel needs. We now live surrounded by the delusions of religion. People must have trust in their leaders, but trust is based on competence, commitment, good communication skills, and ability to build community. The Church rarely attracts to leadership the best anymore.

Many of our current religious leaders are unqualified and unfit or untrained to lead great movements of faith. They are incompetent in those areas in which they should be competent. Numbers and quality of vocations are down, and good Catholic parents no longer want their sons and daughters to be priests or religious. The same workload is now distributed among fewer ministers in what can only be called an organized neglect of the people. It is true that there are so many good ministers struggling in ever more difficult and depressing situations—unappreciated and facing discouragement and erosion of spirit.

Clearly, there are plenty of vocations in the Church and an obvious increase in the spirit of service, but *the administration has chosen celibacy and male exclusiveness over its responsibility to preach the Word and celebrate the Eucharist.* Clergy vocations are coming either from foreign countries for which priestly position is an increase in social status, or from increasingly conservative, insecure, and at times arrogant men who find refuge and security in priestly ministry. The Church has chosen "skilled incompetence" and the effects are evident. Many no longer have the skills needed for a life-giving ministry. They pretend to teach and the faithful pretend to obey. On Sundays, we struggle to understand the English of some individuals, some of whom seem afraid of the future and at most help the administration maintain a semblance of normality while neglecting the real needs of the faithful. Some such dedicated but needy ministers are hardly problem solvers and most certainly not creative guides for a Church of the future. They are sure of themselves but no one else is. They manage the belief systems of their superiors but this does not foster faith.

Great institutions in the Church are shadows of what they could be. It is heartbreaking to see contemporary "leaders" floundering around in their lack of competence, integrity, and ministerial effectiveness, often struggling for short term gain at other people's cost, loss, and pain. Others are hung up on ideological points, often non-essentials, while losing sight of the original vision of their organization. The Church's central teachings today no longer deal with the heart and head but with the pelvic area—gender, homosexuality, abortion, contraception, and all matters sexual. This Catholic "pelvic theology" was not central to Jesus' teachings nor is it to faith. Increasing numbers of the faithful have no intention of listening to this every Sunday and either go elsewhere or stay home. Still other ministers arrogantly think they know what is best for their followers, when everyone knows that managers in any organization, including the Church, are responsible for most of the mistakes in any organization. Many of our "leaders" are not what we need, and we spend more time and energy trying to get rid of, or manage, unqualified leaders than we do trying to cultivate good ones. As a result, nowadays, so many followers simply ignore their so-called leaders, work hard to manage their leaders' defects, and shop around for a spiritual leader in the yellow pages or on Facebook. Let us face it, most of the people we call leaders are at best good managers with a sprinkling of inspiration now and again.

Rather than being served by leaders, we often identify our leaders as oppressive forces who put shackles on the powerless and *stunt religious growth*. New, young, and inexperienced clergy come to a new parish, ignore the gains of years, and impose their conservative agenda on the faithful. In the middle ages the citizens were allowed one day a year when they made fun of their leaders; it was called "The Feast of Fools." Nowadays, it would be a daily event, as our organizations are laid waste by those who claim to lead us.

In the past, ministers were the sources of knowledge of the faith, inspiration in challenging to faith, community leaders, spiritual guides, and liturgical leaders. It is rare to find these gifts today and faith suffers. We used to quote Scripture of our ministers; "I have filled him with the spirit of God and endowed him with skill" (Ex 31:3). It is a rare combination today. In many organizations, leader pathology is a serious problem and trying to collaborate with such unbalanced people is painful for believers with values. So many, good dedicated Christians, like many in other religions, live unfocused and misguided lives because of *poor direction, guidance, and leadership*. Our world is complex and also sinful, and some of the worst situations are the result of the failure of public figures, even in the Church. Spiritual leaders are always living in the shadow of pathological leaders who have no sense of fidelity, or justice, or dedication to service, or direction for the

Church. Good Christians must maintain self-control and not accept the failures of others but rather offer an alternative way of living in contemporary society.

Moral bankruptcy

"Their hearts are astray, these people do not know my ways" (Ps 44:10)

If religion and its leaders only suffered from irrelevance it might not be so bad, but religion faces increasing accusations of corruption, avarice, sexual abuse, infidelity, political power-plays and other sins that leave good church-goers struggling to save their faith. The Church in almost every country has faced tragedies, and *believers and disbelievers alike have been shocked and scandalized* at just how bad leaders in the Catholic Church have been and still are. The United States Church has had to deal with pedophilia, abuse, death in its orphanages and schools, corruption, criminal activities in its bishops, misuse of the people's money, sick careerism, and political and religious hypocrisy – and the list grows.

We looked forward with enthusiasm to Pope Francis' dedication to reform and no one can doubt his efforts, but results are not as evident as many had hoped. Even supporters of Pope Francis point out he has the authority but after several years little to show for it on an organizational level. *The pope has met with enormous opposition from conservative bishops* as well as from members of the Curia and their administrative offices who want to preserve the status quo with its corruption, luxury, and hidden agendas. The Pope recently described reforming the Church as more difficult than cleaning the Egyptian pyramids with a toothbrush (Christmas Message to the Curia, 2017). In his message to the Curia, Pope Francis spoke about a few members of the Vatican administration who are doing enormous damage to the Church. In a series of criticisms presented with surgical precision he referred to the cancer of cliques, "traitors of confidence," "those who take advantage of the motherly concerns of the Church," and "those who allow themselves to be corrupted by ambition and vanity." The Pope lamented that after he eases traitors out without making a fuss of their failures, they then present themselves as martyrs, badly treated by the old guard or by a pope who is out of touch. Everyone in attendance knew to whom the Pope was referring.

Pope Francis has made major efforts at reforming the Curia and used his Christmas addresses as continual challenges and rebuke. In previous addresses, especially Christmas 2014, *the Pope listed problems with the Curia.* Among his criticisms, he accused the members of feeling they were indispensable, lacking in self-criticism, and being spiritually and mentally hardened. He said the participants worked on their own with no coordination, were rivals rather than collaborators, and suffered from spiritual Altzheimers. He accused participants of hypocrisy and existential schizophrenia in which their bureaucratic responsibilities were separate from their spiritual lives. The Pope lamented the "terrorism of gossip," careerism and opportunism, indifference to others, presenting images of sadness that result from sterile pessimism, fear, and insecurity. The Pope also expressed how sad he was to see the members constantly accumulating material goods and power. Elsewhere, Pope Francis has spoken of "open resistance," "hidden resistance," and "malicious resistance." These comments form the Pope's assessment of the principal leaders in the Church. In his authoritative call for reform he is increasingly alone.

On the occasion of Pope Francis' visit to Chile (January 2018), under the title "The Church resists Francis' efforts regarding liberation theologians," *the authors catalogued the persecutions of theologians by the Congregation for the Doctrine of Faith* and by bishops in whose dioceses there are Catholic universities. They showed how the pre-modern structures of the Church act as if each part is an absolute monarch. The authors' comment on the violations of human rights and the lack of due process, the loss of positions, and pressures of all kinds. They claim there remains a climate of fear and a war against Pope Francis.[1]

A self-righteous trend among some Cardinals and their supporters indicates they think they know what is needed in the Church but they do not think the Pope does. Having called the faithful to obey their pastors, a few arrogant Cardinals and some local bishops' conferences claim they are right and they must "fraternally correct" the Pope. Of course they never felt this need with the Pope's conservative predecessors and their lack of fidelity to the teachings of the Vatican Council. They and their supporters suggest the Pope is not focusing on his main obligations, especially to be a support for his brethren. Rather, his critics feel he has created an image of a good pope and a bad Curia, and they resent it. However, his critics give the impression that obedience is fine for the faithful to their bishops but not for bishops in relationship to the Pope. *Some bishops and cardinals either have little knowledge of, or interest in, authentic collegiality.* They find this lack of faith to be particularly convenient in distancing themselves from the papal challenges. It is sad to see the pain of Pope Francis as he struggles to reform the Church and finds so much opposition from those who should support him, especially from those closest to him. The so-called Church leaders' lack of faith and commitment to the Church's common belief system is stunning. These leaders of the Church evidence the opposite of faith. What are the faithful meant to do? Is the best we can do simply to believe in spite of Church leaders?[2]

In the scandal-ridden Vatican leaks have become more common, since many members' commitment is not to the Church or to the Pope, but to themselves or their cliques. Secret documents have been stolen by Vatican representatives, members of the Vatican imprisoned, and the financial mismanagement, waste, and abuse made public. Pope Francis has tried to reform Vatican finances and the Vatican bank. A group of international auditors informed the Pope that there was *no transparency in Vatican finances*. Cardinals benefitted from luxury apartments for next to no rent, had servants and luxury limousines paid for by the Church, diverted funds from Peter's Pence and children's hospital funds to renovate luxury penthouse suites for themselves. The problems were, and continue to be, endless.

In early March, 2018, a special insert to the official Vatican newspaper, *L'Osservatore Romano*, reported on confidential interviews of nuns who work as domestic servants to bishops and cardinals. *These interviews documented the oppression of nuns in the Vatican.* The nuns stated they had no contracts, no stable hours of work, endless work, very poor pay, and were undervalued in their religious vocations. They referred to their positions as "one of the great thefts of history," and several said they lived in fear. The writer said "clericalism is still killing the Church." One sister said when she was ill the cleric she had served for thirty years never even visited her. Others were sent away without a single word of explanation or justification, and another claimed "we are witnessing a true abuse of power," "women are made invisible."

The Pope set up *a super-congregation to oversee all Vatican finances*. He receives little support and has had little success. The Cardinal in charge is now embroiled in problems of cover-up of sexual abuse and rampant pedophilia and has had to take a leave of absence from the Vatican to defend himself. Pope Francis also set up a Special Commission for the reform of the Curia, made up of nine cardinals, and led by a trusted friend, a man known for his pronouncements on poverty and his support of the poor. At the end of 2017 the Pope discovered his friend was awash in millions of dollars, had been receiving a monthly stipend of 35,000 euros from a University in Honduras, and had put millions of diocesan funds in questionable investments with no reporting. Those in attendance said the Pope just put his head in his hands, saddened yet again by the betrayal of those in whom he had placed his trust. Instead of seeing the spiritual witness of his closest associates he must read books and articles that list all the financial holdings, investments, art works, and properties of his millionaire cardinals. The Pope, in a meeting with laity who work in the Vatican, commented, "This is a problem of conscience for me; we can't preach the social doctrine of the Church and then do the things that are being done."[3]

Many clergy and religious in the Roman Catholic Church have earned and continue to earn *a reputation for sexual abuse* especially pedophilia; an assessment that has unfortunately tainted all. Dioceses around the world have had to declare bankruptcy to cover the costs of claims by abused people who have suffered for years. There have been many cases of individual priests guilty of horrendous crimes and cover-ups by bishops and Vatican officials. There have also been reports of systematic sexual abuse of students in colleges, schools, and orphanages all over the world. As one example, a Royal Commission in Australia declared in their 2017 report that several thousand children had been raped or abused primarily by Catholic priests in the last ten years. In August, 2018, the attorney general of Pennsylvania reported that a grand jury found over a thousand cases of sexual abuse by over three hundred predatory priests. In the days following the report, many more cases were reported and local authorities concluded there were probably several thousand victims. Within days, other states' attorneys general indicated they were opening grand juries or committees to examine clergy sexual abuse.

Besides these cases and other gross abuses in the USA and Canada, at least six *Europe countries have suffered major revelations of sexual perversion by clergy.* In September, 2018, Germany's Catholic bishops released the findings of a four year study that concluded at least 3,766 children had been sexually abused by at least 1,602 Catholic priests between 1946 and 2014. Other countries that so far have hidden the information will surely be highlighted in the years ahead. Then we will have to report on the sexual abuse of women including nuns by clergy in various countries notably several African countries. Pope Francis and good dedicated clergy, religious, and laity have striven to resolve these problems, but the problems are so great and extensive they cannot get a handle on the problem let alone resolve it. Little will change until women are in key leadership roles in the Church and until there are radical changes in the selection and seminary training of male candidates for the priesthood.

Pope Francis struggles to deal with the issue, but even he *at times gives mixed messages.* In the last weeks of 2017 he officiated at the funeral of the former Cardinal of Boston, who had to leave his diocese in disgrace over his attempted cover-up of pedophilia. Outrage followed the Pope's presence at this funeral and commentators pointed out that the cardinal had the Pope at his funeral while good Christians are thrown out of the Church after a second marriage, forbidden communion if they have an abortion, politicians criticized for supporting the law of the land, and religious disgraced for promoting women's issues. The Pope's suggestion that divorcees could receive communion led to a firestorm of dissent. Even now, dioceses have short lists of reserved sins that affect the laity, but the clergy have been largely untouched and unpunished. The contrast was offensive to so many. In just days following the cardinal's special send-off, the Pope discontinued the committee on sexual abuse that he had founded. Fortunately, he reinstated it some months later. The Church struggles for integrity and faith-based living and does not always find it.[4]

As we think about our desire to have faith-filled lives that manifest their values in beliefs and share them with others in community, it is hard to do this when we think about the failures of Church leaders. *No one can live in the way many of these people do and at the same time have a living faith.* After corruption, hypocrisy is the key failure of many leaders. The Church has always had leaders who have poisoned the Church's mission and used their position for personal gain, but we seem to be going through a particularly bad period when so-called leaders refuse to respond to the Pope's call for renewal and reform and embody failings that are diametrically opposed to faith. We place our hope in the Church but often we see no vision of hope in its leaders and so much of our hope is little justified. When stress is generated by frustrated hope the organization must expect departures of followers. If our leaders are to be credible they must keep our hope alive. Nowadays, we need leaders who have enthusiasm, can inspire the community, and can maintain stability and dedication to the shared values of faith.

As we strive to deepen faith, nurture our belief, and work with dedicated others in community, we are also surrounded locally, nationally, and internationally, by people who degrade our faith, are selective in their beliefs, live outside shared religious values, and seem to have agendas of their own. All this makes it harder to believe and to focus on faith. Looking at the big picture can be disheartening and raises serious questions of credibility. Let us maturely acknowledge failings in our midst, avoid discouragement, fight to remove them, and recommit ourselves to the Lord who is the source and authentication of faith.

Personal reflection

The history of the Church is punctuated with periods when Church leaders become irrelevant to the community's faith-filled members, either because of the meaninglessness of their message, lack of qualifications, disregard of spiritual renewal, or simply their own faithlessness and sin. I think we are in such a period today, when believers do not look to hierarchy or clergy in general for spiritual guidance, moral direction, integrity, or vision for a spiritual Church of the future. Many are left in disillusionment, apathy, indifference, and discouragement. Where are they to go?

Questions for discussion or personal reflection

1. Where will the Church find leaders for today and tomorrow?

2. How do the many scandals of recent years challenge your faith? What suggestions do you have for solving the scandals that plague the Church?

3. Do you think that at times we simply forget who we are supposed to be as Christians?

Chapter Three
RELIGION WITHOUT FAITH

Worrying trends and the absence of faith

"You . . . have neglected the weightier matters of the law, justice and mercy and faith" (Mt 23:23)

O ur faith is based on our conviction that God has chosen to enter our lives and transform us and our world into a vision of love. This experience governs everything we do. It implies an ongoing conversion, a letting go of old ways, and an opening of ourselves to lives built on love. Hopefully, with St. Paul we can say, "I live by faith in the Son of God, who loved me and gave himself for me" (Gal 2:20). This profound transforming vision is frequently replaced by a bumper-sticker set of values and goals that lead us away from true faith, life-giving beliefs, and an enriching community.

There is an increasing disconnect between some Christians' stated beliefs and their daily lives. Many claim to base their lives on faith in a loving God but their churches produce the opposite of what they claim. Jesus reminded us that by their fruits you will know them. They are addicted to protecting their own interests and evidence racist approaches to blacks, Hispanics, or immigrants. They are regular church-goers who emphasize the importance of the Bible as the foundation of life but live a cultural and spiritual pathology of opposition to others' growth and fundamental rights. They presume they are part of a dominant class. Some find justification in reading out of context a few Old Testament texts that support their views of a chosen race. Yet, some are content with their lives, even religiously defend their way of viewing society, and seem to make Christianity and the cross means of domination.

Believers cannot live in ways that are incompatible with the vision of Christianity. This disconnect leads *some individuals and groups to substitute non-Christian values and agendas for those that should emerge from faith.* This produces artificial lives in people who seem shackled to the wrong vision and to the wrong God. This contemporary apostasy from genuine Christianity is found, among others, in political leaders who present themselves as Christian, or specifically Roman Catholic, but constantly pursue policies opposed to Catholic social teachings and the Christian pursuit of justice. In this context the preaching of the values of a market-based economy, the advantages of capitalism, growth based on trickle-down economics, preservation of gross inequalities, and an ethics of self-sufficiency are all opposed to gospel values that seek justice, compassion, and the common good. This they do while enriching their own lives with exorbitant salaries, benefits, healthcare, and pensions. There is no faith at all in much of what leaders in politics, business, and healthcare present as major social goals. Moreover, partisanship has blinded many to the fundamental difference between right and wrong. What we see nowadays in some groups is social, institutionalized, and religiously supported sin.

Unfortunately *we live surrounded by the devout hypocrisy* of people who, while claiming to be believers, are immersed in bigotry. Where is their faith? Some of the most successful churches and religious leaders are those that feed on each other's bigotry. We are creating future generations of hate and violence. Intolerance is an aspect of religious purity that seeks isolationism, separating walls, better-than-thou attitudes, and ultimately religious wars—as we see all around the world. Outsiders looking at people who speak of faith might well conclude that Christianity's time and usefulness has ended. Even for the dedicated, life in the Church is no longer attractive and in many cases does not advance Christ's agenda or our personal faith. When divisiveness predominates, it is hard for believers to deepen awareness of their own responsibility to constantly seek means to resolve disputes in a manner worthy of followers of Christ.

A parallel approach to these examples of growing irrelevance and distancing of selves from authentic values is *the practice of consoling people in their irrelevance and failures* instead of challenging them. So, we have ever increasing numbers of preachers, TV presenters, mega-churches, and social and religious strategists who encourage their followers to fight for their non-evangelical values, to maintain the status-quo, and to continue to impose their own laws and practices on others. All these sources of encouragement need enormous financial support for their leaders, most of whom seem to have forgotten Jesus' calls for poverty and sharing. There are very few successful preachers and religious leaders who are poor. There is too much money in religion in the United States. Francis of Assisi was a lone voice for "lady poverty" in his time, as is Pope Francis in ours. Where is faith? What are the values we stand for?

We have seen that many religious leaders have failed us and continue to do so. Leaders can get away with a lot if they have charisma, control of the finances, and if their followers are insecure. We have seen that *many so-called Christians no longer need their so-called leaders to be ethical.* In fact, several are not. They just need them to be dedicated to the ultra-conservative, discriminatory, social sexual agenda that followers like. Followers need the support of a leader's ideology more than his or her integrity. So, we see the ever present spiritual dictatorships and barren proclamations. There is no faith in any of this.

Religious language without faith

"This people honors me with their lips but their hearts are far from me" (Mk 7:6)

The use and abuse of religious language by social, political, educational, and parental groups has always been a common practice. It helps to affirm positions and practices, claim political boundaries, justify social and education goals, and influence lifestyles. Nations have claimed that God gave them their land, rulers have insisted to be anointed by God with the divine rights of kings, crusades have been launched in God's name, religious leaders have claimed absolute obedience based on the fact that they represent God, other people's lands have been stolen and their people enslaved, great and minor lords and ladies have claimed ownership of their people in a divinely established feudal system, and abbots and other religious leaders have insisted on total obedience since they claimed to be ruling in the place of God. God has been blamed for a lot of human abuse over the centuries.

Countries all over the world continue to do these things, notably the United States of America. Presidents of the United States whether religious or irreligious, moral or immoral, servants or dictators, believers or atheists, always end any statement of major policy, proclamation of war, even annual speeches or reports, with a fervent hope that God may bless America. "God Bless America" is one of our favorite anthems or hymns, our coins declare "In God we Trust," and Sunday church-going is socially obligatory in many states. *Our politicians are steeped in meaningless religious language* during campaigns and like to be seen attending religious functions. National leaders view the United States as good and other countries as bad, and their policies at times give the impression that we good guys are ridding the world of evil. Other countries and their leaders are referred to as bad, they are demonized, and viewed together as some kind of "axis of evil," while in the United States we feel comfortable referring to "American exceptionalism," and many often see the nation as specially blessed by God.

Religious language is common in fighting threats to the American way of life, whether such threats come from communism, feminism, immigration, Islam, or the environmental movement. Dialogue is considered unacceptable, and "compromise" a dirty word. Christians are called to dominate the world and American Christians must take the lead on a world scale—views readily supported by many ideological leaders. We are told that the fact that the United States is a wealthy nation is a sign of God's blessing and approval of its fight for values and no one should be ashamed of this theology of prosperity.

The United States lectures the world on human rights, even though its own failures are extensive. It presents itself as the standard bearer of justice, a Christian country with Christian values that seeks to influence and win over or force other countries to its ways. With these values the United States is the guarantee of good world order and sees itself as an outstanding Christian country—just look at the percentage of church-goers!

Many years ago *we were warned about "bourgeois religion"— religion with social agendas but no vision of faith*. Today many people who go to Church do so satisfied with their own lives, values, and involvements. They go to church to have their approach to life "religiously endorsed and rounded off . . . protected and strengthened by religion" (17)[5]. This blessing and sanctioning of what we already have and are, never needs to confront the challenges of faith, rather the latter is in grave danger. Faith should disrupt our comfortable lifestyles not endorse them.

Church going is an important social activity, a chance to meet friends, show off nice clothes, and contribute to a collection for worthy causes. It is also, a time for good music and an encouraging sermon with a little challenge, but not too much, and an opportunity for a little programmed spontaneity when appropriate. Religious language must be used well to foster a little prayer, to nurture beliefs, and to explain the Scriptures as supporting pre-conceived positions, but it is rarely threatening. There is little or no significant change of heart, or radical conversion in our churches. People who attend Church often lack a fundamental option for the values of faith. People do not leave different than when they entered. *Genuine conversion "is being obscured by the appearance of a mere belief in faith"* (19). We can say we believe all kinds of things without changing our lives— religious talk is cheap. At the end of the service we can receive our certificate of attendance and go home consoled. However, religious language is not faith, and much of Christianity that we see "publicly proclaimed and ecclesiastically prescribed and believed in" (20) is simply a bourgeois religion.

Churches today are frequently the people's Churches. The people own them and their values and vision—all which gives the attendees the security they seek. Gradually, *world values overwhelm the Church* and then instead of the Church influencing society, it is the latter that influences the Church and at times overwhelms it. Then repentance and discipleship are managed carefully and become secondary to the comfortable practices of the faithful.

The bourgeois Church we now have restricts virtue to the narrow private confines of family or celibate groups, and public virtue tends to be equated with money and occasional battles or perhaps skirmishes over sexual and political issues—something tangible that we can congratulate ourselves about. Members tend to maintain the Church not by virtuous living but by money and political and social involvement. Young people do not identify with this bourgeois Church and drift away, not because the Church demands too much but because it expects too little. To pursue *genuine discipleship means abandoning this bourgeois Church we have become*, and to many that will appear as betrayal and treason to what they have created. But if we want to pursue faith can we remain immersed in this religious language without spiritual substance?[6]

In God we trust—really!

"And many false prophets will arise and lead many astray"
(Mt 24:11)

Recent decades have seen a mixing of politics, morals, and religion to the detriment of faith, many religious leaders have entered politics to promote their religious views, and others have thwarted all kinds of good social and political policies in their battles to impose one issue of their religion's agenda, and in doing so have deprived millions of needy people of the aid they lacked.

Politics all over the world, including the United States, is now less a struggle for the common good, and more a battle to impose one social and religious view on everyone. Politicians, educators, hospital management, judges, and religious leaders must all meet the litmus tests of increasingly zealous and angry devotees of one religious tradition or another. If approved, they can expect their supporters to invest lots of money—even on the dark web—to make sure they are elected or supported. Religion is now used to divide rather than to unite us in God's vision of love. In the divisiveness that followed the Reformation different regions solved their differences with the idea "Cuius regio eius et religio" "you must follow the religion of the one who rules." Nowadays, States, social, political, and even business groups strive to impose their religious views on those people in their areas of influence.

These approaches are seen in their clarity in positions such as white Christian Evangelical fundamentalism and extreme conservative Roman Catholicism, among others. *Both have sought to bring their moral influence to affect the political process in favor of their views.* Both have received criticism for their narrow views of morality—mainly sexual issues, and for the brainwashing of their followers who pursue single issues like the fight against abortion or homosexuality, or restricting of minority voting rights as if they were the essence of the gospel. Towards the end of 2017 over three hundred professors of theology in their annual meeting (AAR and SBL) condemned the lack of evangelical values in the current white Christian Evangelical fundamentalism. Moreover, the leadership of Southern Evangelicals was viewed very badly in its pathetic defense of the Alabama Republican candidate, accused of multiple cases of sexual abuse. In a TV interview in January 2018, Michael Steele, former RNC chair, expressed outrage at evangelical leaders' giving Trump "a mulligan" over allegations he paid a porn star. Steele commented, "I have a very simple admonition at this point. Just shut the hell up and don't ever preach to me about anything ever again. I don't want to hear it." He added, "After telling me how to live my life, who to love, what to believe, what not to believe, what to do and what not to do, and now you sit back and the prostitutes don't matter? The outrageous behavior and lies don't matter? Just shut up."

Conservative Roman Catholicism has also been criticized for its narrowing of policy and ministry goals to pelvic issues. In both cases, *gone are the values of the great Christian teachings like those in the Sermon on the Mount.* Both groups evidence intolerance towards other views, attack opponents with religious zeal, claiming tax exemptions while making millions, and both supported Donald Trump as president. Neither needed Trump to have integrity, moral standing, or empathy for the poor and oppressed—in fact, they knew he did not. They just needed to know he would support their agenda of fighting abortion, opposing gay and other minority rights, keeping the country pure, maintaining religious influence in education, and appointing conservative activist judges throughout the country and especially in the Supreme Court. Some religious groups claim to base their ideas on Scripture, but they do not, and they lack solid connections to faith, having abandoned genuine faith-based doctrine for fringe issues that do not reflect the memory of Jesus.

These groups and others like them are committed to a spiritual war. They manipulate their own members in the name of authentic religion—no communion to divorced, or to those who support abortion, gay marriage, women priests, and they withdraw support from political candidates who espouse these issues. A serious problem for these warring religious groups is their agendas were not Jesus' agenda. *Most of the topics for which they fight were not mentioned by Jesus in his preaching.* They have religious views and transient beliefs that are not expressions of a faith-filled encounter with a loving God. What is to happen to these pseudo faith-based groups?

Many Christians seem to have gone astray or been led astray, away from the core values that result from faith and are expressed in a belief system that reflects the values of love that is the basis of faith. It would be nice if Christians pursued a mission, values, justice, a sense of purpose, the common good, and hope—all resulting from the love experienced in faith and grounded in Scripture. Love is the epiphany of God, and we need Christians whose profession is universal love. Love should transform our inner lives and lead to mercy towards others. This love cannot be "a merely believed-in love" that calms and consoles, and allows Christians to continue their "untroubled believing" with their backs to the realities of contemporary life. Christianity is not just a doctrine to which we give intellectual assent; it is "a praxis to be lived radically." Faith results from God's interventions in our lives. We are not only passive in receiving this grace but must also express it in daily life; we must "enact" our faith in the way we live.[7]

Christianity is a work of supreme love for others, and it cannot co-exist with what we are seeing in many churches today. When we reject compassion and uplifting help to others it undoes God's loving mercy to us and violates the experience of faith in God's universal love. Let us carefully protect the essence of our faith.

Personal reflection

I feel I must acknowledge that religions in general and Christianity and Roman Catholicism in particular have lost their way. Gospel values are not the priority but sexual, social agendas,

power, money, and their controlling impact on people, especially
women. Christian churches and traditions today do not preach
Jesus' priorities but their own. We are left asking whether
Christianity can survive the current abuse and neglect.

Questions for discussion or personal reflection

1. How can we get rid of these burdens on our faith?

2. What can you do to make sure your faith can survive the current
abuse and neglect.

3. What should happen to those religious leaders who betray the
faith?

Chapter Four

DOES THE CHURCH CARE ABOUT WHAT YOU CARE ABOUT?

Major concerns of dedicated believers

"Whatever you do, work at it with all your heart, as though you were working for the Lord, and not for [people]" (Col 3:23)

D oes the Church as an institution promote our search for deeper faith? Do we, called to be living witnesses of Christ's presence, promote the search for deeper faith? Can we find God in today's religion? Does the Church as the great channel of God's grace actually care about what we care about? Many Roman Catholics are deeply disturbed and troubled about the direction of the Church and its lack of support in faith development. It often seems the organization of the Church gives more emphasis to itself than to Jesus or the sacraments. It no longer seems that the Church cares about what they care about.

Increasing numbers are disgusted with the Church's failures. Some are fed up and even angry, and they withdraw their loyalty to the organization that at one time was central to their contentment and hope. Here are several major subjects that dedicated believers have told me they care about. It is not the result of a scientific poll but the result of involvement with large and small groups of believers all over the world—from hundreds of programs I have given in 35 States, 5 Canadian Provinces, and 15 other countries. Readers can reflect on these issues and their importance in life and judge whether these are the issues that are important in their lives.

A constant request of people who want to grow in faith is that the Church *give priority to spiritual growth*, which in many cases it does not. In spirituality for the most part we wander around, disoriented and dissatisfied. It seems that the Church is too easily satisfied with the small spiritual challenges it offers. The innumerable practices of piety accepted over the years have not led to spiritual growth or union with God for most believers. Even the saints the Church presents to us seem more old fashioned controls over popular piety than great inspirers and examples of spiritual renewal for the future. The Church's year offers outer changes for each season, pre-packaged religion, a predictable display of annual piety. After going to Church every Sunday for 20, 30, 40, and even 50 years, many Catholics firmly confess that they are bored with its piety and often just tune out. Believers want inner transformation, a guided dedication in the human search for meaning and for God. This will require an entire redoing of the Church's spiritual system. We suffer from a tragic loss of spiritual depth, heroic lives, exemplary leaders and mystical encounter. How do we deepen faith in these circumstances? Can people who do not seem to know the Church teach us how to encounter God?

Believers love the Church but want meaningful growth and are *saddened by constant decline in the Church.* Many state they do not feel nourished when they go to Church and feel closer to God at other times of the day more than when in Church. While they acknowledge that they used to find nourishment and guidance from clergy or religious, they now find it with spouse, friends, even Facebook connections. Trickle-down religion is finished for serious seekers, and for many believers the Church is a shadow of what it used to be. Instead of finding resources, vitality, challenge, spiritual energy, and a sense of spiritual and ministerial direction, increasing numbers of believers experience disappointment and friction and these experiences lead to a loss of commitment. We all know that hierarchical structures generally tend to preserve the status quo, but they are losing their grip and lay faithful are becoming more self-directed as they lament the loss of the Church's importance in their lives of faith.

People who long to grow in faith wish for *more emphasis on Jesus Christ*, the source of faith, rather than on the Church organization. We seem to get more teachings about the Church than we do about Jesus. Faith in a loving God and in the life and death of the Son helps keep in perspective the smallness and at times pettiness of the Church. Scripture shows that Jesus is the answer to our yearnings, but more and more we are faced with the arrogance of religion that thinks it has the answers. The organizational Church needs to rethink its role and re-strategize to attain its real goals.

Often believers, members of the Church, have a more profound understanding of what the organization's role in their lives ought to be than do members of the inner administration of the organization. Believers want the Church to *teach the right things*—prayer growth, union with God, baptismal life, vocation and responsibility, the centrality of the Eucharist, justice, service, and community love. There is too much mouthed prayer, empty reflection, programmed spontaneity, artificial attitudes, hypocritical piety, and merely believed-in love. The purpose of all religion is to lead us to God. The Sermon on the Mount is primarily a statement on the integrity and authenticity of religious values. Unfortunately, many believers find they have not been led to encounter God, nor experienced these values, nor been led in appropriate spiritual renewal in their local churches. If we were to ask non-Catholics in the United States, or even Catholics for that matter—what are the central teachings of the Catholic Church, we all know what they would say and their answers would not be what Jesus hoped they would be. Their answers would certainly not focus on growth in the experience of faith.

Included in the desire that the Church teach the right things is the insistence that the Church stand up for the poor and *proclaim the social teachings of the Church*. In Jesus' inaugural sermon he said that working for the poor was his great priority (Lk 4:18), and when John the Baptist asked for a clarification of Jesus' ministry Jesus' answer was to look at what he did for the poor and oppressed (Mt 11:4-5). Christianity offers the world a new set of values, new goals, and new attitudes; those followers who claim to have faith in Jesus must focus their lives on the underprivileged, poor, oppressed, and all outcasts. Dedicated believers want to see the Church live up to Jesus' platform of social justice and societal reform.

Believers *seek meaningful and enriching liturgy*. Good liturgies require someone who speaks our language and understands our culture. The celebrant needs a sense of presence, pastoral skills, genuine interest in the people, and, of course, excellent knowledge of Scripture. Liturgy must use and speak the congregation's language. We see a return to old fashioned language; a renewal of the distancing of priest from people, non-Scripture based homilies, and male dominance. Many priests, and especially deacons, are inadequately trained in liturgical skills and once ordained seem to disdain further study.

A lot of Catholics who became actively involved members of the Church did so with the vision and challenges of the Second Vatican Council. A yearning I hear so much is the desire for *a recommitment to the conciliar values.* This desire contrasts with the bizarre reactions of the Vatican Curia who have done everything they could to undermine Vatican II. Those same Church insiders now also close ranks as if they were under siege and silently oppose the Pope, as they did the Council, by doing nothing. Over the four years of the Council we witnessed three major attitudinal changes—a genuine conversion of the Church. The Church saw itself as community rather than just an institution. It realized it must incarnate itself in the real world rather than being withdrawn. The Church also saw that it must undertake the mission of service at all levels of its life. Community, incarnation, and service were the hallmarks of the conciliar renewal. It would be great to see them again.

Most laity in the Church along with many clergy and religious want to see *women given their due role in the Church.* We need to see women in key leadership roles. Does anyone think we would have had the gross crimes of pedophilia and cover-ups if women were in key roles? They would not have done or covered up what men have. We also need women in teaching roles, liturgical leadership, administration and government in order to see complementarity, new styles of leadership, and a new vision of Church. Other Churches that have examined the issue with diligence and pursued it with a desire for fidelity have women priests. Roman Catholic opposition seems based more on power and exclusiveness than faith. Vatican and Curial images are meaningless in our contemporary world. At times it is sad to see all elderly cardinals and other old men dressed in their silk and satin robes and all the other trappings of power. It is not a meaningful image of the Church.

Anyone who focuses on deepening personal faith would like to *get money taken out of the Church*. The Church will always need money for charity and ministerial goals. However, the Church should not be a place for corruption, careerism, triumphalism, and greed—and unfortunately it is. Believers do not want to see this kind of Church and yet it goes on and on. There are many in the Church administration who live complex lives with a great deal of integrity, generosity, and personal simplicity. However, there is too much money available to others who corrupt the Church with their greed.

These concerns, cares, and hopes of laity, if addressed, would foster faith in the vision of a loving God. Their neglect is yet another problem for people of faith and makes believing harder than it used to be. These concerns are primarily those of adult laity and would need to be complemented by the insights and experiences of youth ministers and by adequate responses to the concerns and hopes of young people in the Church.

Jesus' priorities

"Why do you not understand what I say? It is because you cannot accept my word" (Jn 8:43)

A new spirit is stirring in the Church, and it can help us deepen our faith. We must overcome the failures of the past and prepare ourselves for a future of growth and responsibility. While many have left the institutional churches, and sadly may never return, perhaps the challenge to renewal of Pope Francis may re-attract them to the essentials of Christian commitment. As an antidote to all we have lost in our pursuit of deeper faith by emphasizing secondary issues, we need a fresh commitment to the priorities of Jesus. Let us rekindle spiritual insight, accept our spiritual destiny, and refocus on the essential teaching of salvation. Let us ask ourselves if these priorities of Jesus are our own or whether they are the priorities of today's Church.[8]

The most important priority in Jesus' life and teachings was to *convey to every person how much God loves everyone*. Jesus came to the world filled with the Father's love in order to share that love with each of us. "For God so loved the world that he gave his only Son, so that everyone who believes in him may not perish but may have eternal life" (Jn 3:16). However, our world is rapidly becoming a loveless place, and we Christians have to change that by making this priority of Jesus our own. The essence of Christianity is love. God is love. The Trinity lives in mutual love. The Incarnation is part of God's strategy of love. Jesus exemplifies and teaches love. Disciples are called to individual and communal love. This must be seen especially in presenting good news to the poor in the Church's healing ministry, and justice to the marginalized and oppressed. Jesus assures us, "those who love me will be loved by my Father, and I will love them and reveal myself to them" (Jn 14:21). The Church's mission is to portray love to the world.

Another energy of the soul that should be a part of the Church's teaching is *hope* which is also a transforming gift from God. It is not the accumulation of small daily hopes every human being seeks to fulfill. Rather, it is a gift from God that totally changes the way we live. To live in hope, to be people of hope, makes life exciting, fulfilling, and worth living. "May the God of hope fill you with all joy and peace in believing, so that you may abound in hope by the power of the Holy Spirit" (Rom 15:13). People who live without the hope that motivates life become people of despair ("despair" comes from Latin and means no hope). So many people feel lonely, abandoned, and without purpose in life—they are longing for love, faith, and hope. However, we try to remain firm as "prisoners of hope" (Zech 9:12), ever ready to walk through the "door of hope" (Hos 2:15). Hope helps us maintain our attention to the wonderful future that God has prepared for us and offers us. It gives meaning to our present life by reminding us what lies ahead. Hope is the most powerful motivating force for faith. Is this a principal teaching in our local church?

Jesus put his greatest energy into challenging people to *conversion*—changing the minds and hearts of others through his ministry. It was the first topic mentioned by both Jesus and John the Baptist in their public ministries. It is the starting point for all other values or stages in the spiritual life, and one of Jesus' greatest priorities. We are each called to conversion, to dedicate ourselves to discover the direction of life that God has for us. "Very truly, I tell you, anyone who hears my word and believes him who sent me has eternal life, and does not come under judgment, but has passed from death to life" (Jn 5:24). This will need to be a carefully guided process that we approach with humility and maturity. Conversion is not a once and for all event but an ongoing experience that affects everything we do. It is a consequence of faith.

Integrity is the spiritual discipline of always speaking the truth, of making sure we will do what we claim we will do, and of faithfully persevering in our priorities. Integrity must involve every aspect of our lives—personal, relational, organizational, and religious. "Nothing is covered up that will not be uncovered, and nothing secret that will not become known" (Lk 12:2). It means accepting ourselves—what we have been and what we can become. Integrity implies that our core beliefs influence everything we do. What is within us affects what others see. Integrity is the essential component of spiritual faithfulness. Jesus took every possible occasion to emphasize it and decry its absence. In our times, steeped as they are in corruption, superficiality, insincerity, and half-hearted commitment, integrity stands out as one of Jesus' most critical priorities and must be for each of us and for our Church today.

Spirituality refers to the human effort to become a person in the fullest sense of the word and to develop one's authentic self. It is the ordering of our lives so that we continually grow in positive ways. It embraces all of life, leaving nothing out, and makes us all well-balanced, well-integrated human beings. There is nothing more important than spirituality which emphasizes our fidelity to the inner values of our hearts and to our response to God. Spirituality will influence every aspect of our lives. It is that constant call to give ourselves to the priorities of God and to respond to the challenge of continual renewal in life. "If any want to become my followers, let them deny themselves and take up their cross and follow me. For those who want to save their life will lose it, and those who lose their life for my sake will find it" (Mt 16:24-5). This should be a central focus in every Church community.

Among the most important supports that Jesus offers his disciples is that of *community*. Part of discipleship is the call to the fellowship that shares the faith, hope, and love that Jesus brings to the world. Disciples are Jesus' own, the Father's possession, and they have new life in the Spirit. Their mutual love binds them together as the new people of God. Community is the concrete expression of their unity that manifests itself in love. When disciples are united in commitment to Jesus they are "one," as the Father and Jesus are one. Being a Christian means centering one's life on others as we read in the *Acts*; "All who believed were together and had all things in common; they would sell their possessions and goods and distribute the proceeds to all, as any had need" (Acts 2:44-45). In our anonymous and selfish world, we make this great priority of Jesus our own—to build community at all levels of our life. The challenge of faith is always to move away from self-centeredness to center one's life on God and on others.

Discipleship and the call to ministry go together. The same Spirit who calls us to follow Jesus also calls us to ministry in his name. Each one of us has been given his or her own share of grace, given as Jesus willed it. One of Jesus' great priorities is that every follower feels a summons to service—to live, to love, and to labor for the good of others. Faith never allows a passive attitude or a focus on self, but insists that the outpouring of the Spirit is always for the common good. We are all called to the service of each other—that is how the human community grows. Jesus' life culminated with the great mandate to his disciples to go forth in a spirit of service to the whole world, bringing his vision and values to all in order to lead the world to the transformation he came to bring. Disciples are not baptized for themselves but for the service of others in Jesus' name and thus have impact on our world.

Jesus did not come from the Father to serve a particular group of people to the detriment of others. His *concern was for everyone* as seen in his daily lived conviction that every life was precious and that all laws must be secondary to compassion and love. He dealt caringly with people from all walks of life. He was open to welcome all in the Father's name. Our contemporary world desperately needs people who will live a spirituality of universality. We need to reclaim the Christian challenge of universality— striving to understand, accept, share vision, dialogue with, and love all. "Whoever loves a brother or sister lives in the light, and in such a person there is no cause for stumbling. But whoever hates another believer is in the darkness, walks in the darkness, and does not know the way to go, because the darkness has brought on blindness" (1 Jn 2:8-11). When we do this, we find strength and support for our own commitment to universal love and acceptance, and we manifest to others the depth of our faith.

Jesus came from the Father filled with enduring love. He insisted that his goal among us was to bring us fullness of life, which means fullness of love. Now for each of us, the primary purpose of human development is to prepare ourselves for union with God, and we can never be satisfied unless and until we are filled with divine life in loving union. This is the transformation Jesus brings, and this is the transformation we need and seek and to which our faith leads. We will always be restless until we rest transformed in the love of God and until we discover our need in a community of mutual love. Our spiritual journey should lead us towards transformation—to become our best selves, but it must be filled with our efforts, supported by God's grace.

Ten suggestions

"I have prayed for you that your own faith may not fail"
(Lk 22:32)

As we look forward to the Church becoming what it can be, let us look at a few suggestions that will refocus the Church's priorities. With tongue in cheek let us make these suggestions to Pope Francis!

1. Reduce the total number of cardinals to less than 75 and let their nominations be for ten years only. There are currently 180 cardinals with only about 120 eligible to vote for a new pope. Cardinals are supposed to be papal advisors and yet popes consistently ignore many of them and would not follow their advice even if they knew it. Being a cardinal now is status, wealth, prestige, although Pope Francis is trying to change that with his recent appointments. Seeing all the cardinals at a canonization ceremony looks depressing, and many of them no longer contribute to the Church as maybe they used to. We need fewer cardinals and their nominations should be for a limited period of time. To suggest that some of them are important advisors to several popes is simply untrue. Burdening a pope with old men who have been cardinals for years is not fair to a pope. Ten years is more than sufficient. Then let them leave the Vatican altogether and retire.

2. *Establish criteria for the lifestyle of bishops and cardinals, based on poverty, simplicity, knowledge of the Gospel, and spiritual leadership.* Some clergy love status and actively seek it. Princes of the Church, they look archaic in their fancy robes—the Church must cut out all the frills. It should be a spiritual sacrifice and challenge to become a bishop or cardinal. Choosing someone to be a bishop simply because he is fanatical about abortion, opposes women priests, and excoriates against homosexuals has clearly contributed to the decline in the quality of bishops. Canon Law's current descriptions are insufficient. There needs to be serious evaluation of leaders' lifestyles and performance and consequences that matter.

3. *Why not nominate 12 women cardinals?* The only obstacle to this is Canon Law which the Pope can change at will. There is no theological reason not to do this. The fact that it has not so far been done in history is not theologically significant. It is important that Pope Francis do something daring and even drastic to show the importance of women in governance. Start with the nomination of 12 women. Pious platitudes do not cut it anymore regarding the roles of women in the Church.

4. *Reintroduce the practice of the early Church in giving serious consultative voice to leading laity.* This needs to be done at

parish, diocesan, national and international levels. Some Church documents have given lip-service to this idea, but it has never been meaningful in the past. Laity make up over 98% of the Church and together have more to contribute than the remaining 2%. More laity are well trained in Church issues today than are clergy—it is simply a matter of numbers. Clergy need to relinquish their grip on power which is not linked to sacramental life.

5. *Provide the essential liturgy and sacraments to the faithful.* This is the primary obligation of Church officials and it is going unfulfilled. Obviously, it will mean married clergy and women priests. The laity have already accepted these possibilities; it is just the clinging to male supremacy that stops it from happening. Current Church leadership has failed the baptized by depriving them of the Eucharist—the source and center of our unity—and of the proclamation of the Word of God.

6. *Focus on the formation of laity.* In many churches they need training in their knowledge of Scripture. Without serious formation they can drift into literal and unhistorical interpretations which have led and continue to lead many into false views and misdirected lifestyles. Weekly sermons are insufficient, especially when they are not based on Scripture and real life.

7. *Introduce clear procedures for the selection and regular evaluation of all leaders in the Church.* Selection of clergy cannot be left to clergy; it has not worked. Bishops recommending their classmates is totally inappropriate, but common. Selection by laity cannot be worse than what we have had. Moreover, there must be ongoing evaluation—at least every 3-5 years. Decline in education and pastoral effectiveness, along with administrative, psychological, and sexual problems should receive regular review.

8. Train Church personnel to be spiritual guides. We have some bishops who are well-known as business managers, others who are known for their social and interpersonal skills, others who are known for the rigors of their approach to Church power and politics, and more recently others selected as bishops who can control sexual abuse, but not many who are renowned as spiritual leaders. When it comes to spirituality many have no idea what they are talking about. The people's faith development demands their leaders be spiritual guides.

9. Focus on real issues. Many good people leave the Church because it is not meaningful to their lives. That is not the Gospel's fault but the fact that religious leaders often deal in irrelevances. Check what Episcopal conferences talk about, and then ask yourself "who cares a damn?" Look again at Jesus' priorities listed in the previous section. These are the real issues.

10. Change the culture in administrative centers of the Church. Whether it is the Vatican or a diocese anywhere in the world, a center of Catholic organizational life must become a center of spirituality. Many, certainly in the Vatican, but also in dioceses throughout the world, live on islands of irrelevance. Why is it that many old men long to get appointed to sinecures in the Vatican? Christianity and Roman Catholicism in particular must have a clear focus and a firm set of values. Each organizational center must become a center of spirituality. If people do not want to be a part of this, then let them leave. Roman curial officials who need their Mercedes, well-appointed apartments, good income, nuns to clean, serve and cook, should go home.

We have looked at the important concerns and cares of many faithful. We have re-examined Jesus' own clearly established priorities. We ask ourselves if these are the priorities of our local, national, and international Church. What is the Church doing to overcome its failures and refocus to give priority not to itself but to Jesus and his priorities, so that people who search for deeper faith may find it?

Personal reflection

I am increasingly grateful to so many friends, colleagues, acquaintances, and many men and women I do not personally know. They all give witness to the values of faith and support, encourage, and proclaim by their lives the priorities that I too want to make my own. I rarely look to the Church leaders for support, and in some cases I remain profoundly saddened by their lack of inspiration, vision, and ability to make our faith relevant for today.

Questions for discussion or personal reflection

1. What is going to reform the Church, how, and when?

2. Does the Church care about what you care about?

3. If you did not go to Church how would you express your faith?

Chapter Five

STRUGGLING WITH THE CHALLENGES TO FAITH

How can we confront these challenges?

"The Lord looks on those who revere him, on those who hope in his love" (Ps 33:18)

We have been looking at *a series of problems that threaten authentic faith*—that transformation resulting from awareness of God's love for us and for the whole world. Sometimes the confusion that surrounds the three terms—faith, belief, and religion—inevitably leads to wrong focuses and inauthentic lives. Then we viewed the growing irrelevance of modern day religion and its leaders. We looked at the failures that lead people to question the credibility and integrity of those people and institutions that were formerly held in high regard. We considered the misuse of religious language and the decline in faith values in people and institutions that use God, religion, and faith for social and political goals. And finally we asked whether those organizations and people that used to be channels of grace still care about the issues that lead to faith development, and whether they care about what we care about.

Dedicated believers waken up each day and struggle to understand what has happened to the Church they love that used to lead and challenge them to deeper faith. Just when we might think we have figured things out, another scandal hits that throws everything into turmoil again and puts faith on the backburner while we sort out the problems. We acknowledge we all have a notorious capacity to turn small crises into big ones, but even the accumulation of small ones drags us down. Our yearnings for deeper faith in God's love for us and for our world often do not seem to rise to God but waste away within our own hearts—unfulfilled. We have friends who have lost all trust in the Church as an organization that can aid faith and are now reluctant to voice any opposition. But if we do not speak out the irritation can reach a point of explosion, and then we too will be left with no choice but to seek faith development elsewhere, and many are doing this.

If we want to preserve our faith and allow it to grow, then our patient endurance must be illuminated by hope. *We cannot live with an illusion that what we see in the Church today and in the life we are living is all there is.* When we look at the Church's many failings in fostering faith, we cannot fall into hopelessness which can often be symptomatic of our frustration. Rather, negative experiences can, and must, provoke a hope for change. Many disturbing and seemingly hopeless aspects of our Church's failures to foster faith contain hopes, strivings, and desires for some creative response beyond the anguish. This reaction and re-dedication in hope is not easy by any means. We all have friends who have no hope in the Church and its organizations, and to some extent we cannot blame them. Our hope is in Jesus' wishes for a community expression of our response in love. We place our hope in that goal even though it may not be realized in many current expressions of Church.

We must struggle for authentic faith based on Jesus' message and *we fight to prevent the current decline from ultimately changing us*. While we might feel we are no longer on firm ground, our disagreements must not lead to alienation and the tyranny of hopelessness. Frustration, anxiety, worry, and conflict are all the robbers of our inner peace that can destroy our dedication in faith. We often feel paralyzed by the existing order and do not really know how to activate a new order in our life of faith and in our Church. We can add to our hopeful approach by not believing everything negative we hear about the Church, and by not believing everything we immediately think. We may be tempted to overprotection of our own views and opinions. However, like the Great Wall of China and Trump's southern wall, we must remind ourselves that most threats are inside us. A key focus needs to be prudent self-examination.

When the great theologian, Karl Rahner, was asked to address the many problems in the Church that block growth in faith, he responded, *"Where else can we go?"* We cannot deny the groans of the Church, but neither can we get bogged down in the negativity. We must interrupt or disrupt the overwhelming negative evaluations we hear and ask "where else can we go?" We need to savor the suffering we feel and remember the good times that were and that, maybe, can be again—times when the Church was a major channel in faith development.

Unbelief used to be restricted to small groups of intellectuals, or self-styled intellectuals, but now it is widespread even among our friends. It is not always a lack of faith in God but often *many people experience a lack of faith in all the channels that formerly led us to God*. The human search for meaning and for God is part of our very existence. We cannot dodge or avoid the question of faith and of God. But it is hard to follow up on these issues while at the same time rejecting what we thought were the channels of God's grace. We must regain the Church's lost credibility. After all, the Church does not just offer a spirituality of peaceful convenience, but it is a presence that cures the loneliness we never thought we had. It has to become yet again the channel of faith it once was, and this will happen primarily at the grass roots level and percolate up to leaders and administrators.

The Church's Dark Night

"Even the darkness is not dark to you; the night is as bright as the day, for darkness is as light to you" (Ps 139:12)

The problems we experience in the Church today are similar to what the Spanish mystic, John of the Cross, calls a "dark night." A dark night is what happens to a dedicated person in his or her journey to God; a journey in which he or she longs to get to know God more accurately and as a result learn to love God more authentically. John's great interest is to help us journey to God in faith and love, and in doing so show us how to deal with all the ups and downs we might encounter on that journey. The dark night is not the end but the means to live in faith, hope, and love and thus move to union with God. In the experience of the dark night *there comes a point when everything we formerly valued seems to be falling apart.* At such a time, we simply do not know what to do; we feel lost and without a sense of direction, nor does God intervene to help us out. In fact, it seems God has abandoned us or even rejected everything about us. This is not only a description of our own personal journey, but a more than adequate description of the struggles many have in the Church today; we are experiencing a dark night of the Church. It used to be the source and sustainer of faith and now for many no longer is.

The spiritual journey, more than anything else, is the correcting and clarifying of images of God, others, ourselves, our roles in life, our vision and mission and purpose in life—all images that impact who God is for us. *In our current reflections we find the image of the Church needs purification and clarification.* In the dark nights with God's grace we see all this in a new way, but then we must go forth and deliberately look at images of the Church in a new way, until we are left with no further desire for the old ways of relating to God. We cannot abandon the Church God has given to us, but we do let go of the inauthentic images of Church we currently see and experience.

Many readers undoubtedly grew up very comfortable in their Church and possibly responded with enthusiasm to the challenges of renewal in faith. But now many feel strangers in the Church, and find its teachings no longer seem meaningful to them as before and no longer the support of daily life as it used to be. Some Christians, today, stress that they are "conservative" Catholics or "liberal" Catholics, thus emphasizing a particular image they have, an appetite or need, to approach the Church with a particular psychological or sociological focus. *Many dedicated people we know find that today they are outsiders to the Church they have loved so much,* they no longer "practice" by weekly attendance, and they feel that the Church is not as relevant to modern life as they once found it to be. So, many see themselves as Christian and more deeply spiritual than ever, but having formerly found their identity in the Church, they now experience darkness. These same people would love to have leaders they could admire and trust, men and women of profound spiritual commitment, who were genuinely supporters of the faith. These dedicated believers long for a sense of ecclesial vision, experience of community, and spiritual leadership. Unfortunately, they are overwhelmed with problems. We look at our Church and often see big business just as we see in the corporate world. The Church has hospitals, retirement homes, organized charities, social services, and they all look and act just like other NGOs. No matter what the Pope does he cannot get money and corruption out of the organization. However, all these problems do not deal with the essence of the Church, but with images.

In the dark night of our spiritual journey our image of God dies, and God then gives us a new image of divine life. Likewise, with profound sadness we see that *for many believers the former image of the Church is dying*, and many in the Church are attached to sense objects and appetites that need purification as a first step to renewal. It is easy to say the Church is always wonderful and always sinful, but for many nothing seems to change. Rather, they see a helpless clinging to old ways, old images, that needs a passive purification of a dark night for leaders and followers alike, so that the Church can once again satisfy the yearnings of the human heart in a faith-filled experience of God.

Transforming the pain we feel

"I came that they may have life and have it abundantly" (Jn 10:10)

As believers searching for faith we are always uncomfortable. We deal with problems every day and so must be skilled at living with tension. As dedicated believers we feel drawn to our Church and repelled by it at the same time, but we must constantly reaffirm commitment and maintain hope. As believers we know difficulties are an integral part of discipleship, we know we must bear the pain and frustration being a member of the Church brings, and we can manage the discouragement, depression, and rejection that struggling with others produces. So, we look for the good in all that happens, and remind ourselves of how often positive developments result from events that started out negatively. In quiet reflection we focus our hearts on the Church and recommit ourselves to it and to all the struggles that are integral to its achievement. After all, our faith is in God and not in the transitory experiences of the Church.

Let us embrace pain and suffering. As reflective believers we appreciate that suffering is an integral part of the life of a disciple. Generally a person with a sense of destiny has gone through personal suffering and crisis which can often become a source of strength and give the courage to continue. Each of us must be conscious of the pain that surrounds every organization, never inflict pain on others, but embrace pain and suffering, accept it while seeking to remove it from the lives of others. Christian discipleship implies transforming life in spite of suffering. As believers we are often the target of suffering and often have to ignore a lot of negativity, major doses of cynicism, and imposed constraints in order to be faithful to the life to which God calls. If we are tempted to ask when will it all end, we must know it is a permanent part of discipleship. In spite of the suffering we must struggle to energize others in our common service for the life of faith. We must be ready for constant change, take success or failure in stride, and face the future with passion, boldness, and courage. However, even all these efforts will be filled with struggles and pain.

We need to learn to accept failure. If as believers we want to grow in spiritual life then we must learn to live with failure and the pain it brings rather than hiding it or denying it. We must not be anxious when the future does not yield all the change or success we hope for, but must remain calm and peaceful. Our joys and strengths are always linked to needs and miseries that also come along. Every day will have its pains and struggles, in fact, some experiences we must confront seem to suck the life out of us. But each of us needs to accept the limits of our successes and thereby move beyond them. As people dedicated to spiritual growth we also appreciate the gifts of all and establish a new approach to failure for others too, in fact, even welcome it, knowing that anyone who wants to be successful must learn to fail and learn from failing.

Let us strive to bring healing to all organizations that support our faith. There is an intimate link between Christian commitment and healing. As spiritual men and women we focus on integrated, holistic approaches to people and to organizations, removing what is sick and dysfunctional, bringing harmony, striving for wellness, and thus enriching the vision. Believers must first of all repair the harm of the past and the pain it caused, then be aware that all organizations are often sick and dysfunctional, have harmful environments and structures, and become oppressive and destructive. There are many casualties of sick organizations that are filled with disharmony and lack of balance. All this needs healing too. As believers we should review our organizations and discern what needs healing. We should encourage all to live the vision with courage and perseverance. To this end let us cultivate a spirit of reconciliation and compassion in the whole community, let us make it clear what we will accept and what we will not, and let us choose carefully and responsibly in which churches we will participate and share life.

Remember some truths can only be seen in darkness. We live today in dark times for growth in faith and often find it difficult to come up with the right answers or we feel bombarded with answers that turn out to be superficial. Living in times of darkness when nothing seems clear can be a good experience, for darkness helps us block out partial answers, eliminate those which do harm, and it challenges us to think things through more carefully. Darkness can be the beginning of newness of life which is like a dawn. In fact, one can even find what one is looking for even when you are not looking—answers just come effortlessly in dark times and in times of reflection. So, our lives can sometimes be better in darkness, and we should learn to trust times of darkness. What darkness does for us is do away with useless answers that come in partial light; so one can even say that enlightenment comes in darkness. Nothing is ever so bright as when we come out of darkness. The experience of darkness, confusion, and loss comes with entrance into contemplative prayer, when God takes away former securities and replaces them with a darkness that at first obscures and then illumines our way forward.

Be joyful, optimistic, and enthusiastic. Joy, optimism, and enthusiasm are three interconnected concepts in the life of every believer who must struggle with the pains and suffering of our contemporary life and world. We need to be vibrant, cheerful, full of interests, and excited about life. All discipleship has its times of oppression, justified reactions of anger, and feelings of resentment. We have to put up with a lot of negativity and personal criticisms while trying to keep optimistic and to maintain positive motivation of others. Joy is an essential component of the life of every Christian, preceding and concluding every stage in life. Optimism is the attitude of one who takes a hopeful view of things, expects positive outcomes, and looks forward to achieving good developments in the Christian presence in the modern world. Enthusiasm describes a believer who is guided by the values of God (en theos = in God) and can approach his or her work with confidence. These three qualities enable all of us to live with courageous patience, resilience, innovative thinking, openness to the future, and encouraging hope. These qualities call us to go forward in the midst of all the scandals around us, and insist that we still proclaim the vision of hope for which we strive.

We need to be skilled in interrupting the decline we see in the Church's ability to foster and proclaim faith. Instead of being paralyzed by the current situation and its many problems, we must see that many are really preferences that we can change. While savoring the loss we feel and facing up to it, let us regain some of the fire, and passion, and genuine conversion we once had.

Personal reflection

It seems to me that we are living in a critical period for our Church. In early May, 2018, a Gallup report showed only 39% of Catholics in the US attend Church, down from 45% in 2005 and down from 75% in 1955. This affects all age groups, including the elderly who often participate more than others. The Church has lost its meaning and value for the majority of Catholics—over 60%. We are in a crisis and have been for a long time. Crisis comes from a Greek word meaning judgment; it is a time for serious thought and self-examination and decisions to change direction.

Questions for discussion or personal reflection

1. Are you convinced we have the religious leaders to guide us out of the current crises?

2. Do you get discouraged with the problems facing the Church or can you just ignore them and move on? What can you do to remain positive?

3. How do you think young people view the Church today? Which aspects of Church speak to them and which ones do not?

Part II

SEARCHING FOR
REASONS TO BELIEVE

GIVING AN ACCOUNT OF THE HOPE THAT LIES WITHIN US

I t is harder to believe than it used to be, and in part one we looked at some of the trends in our world and in religion that make it harder. We looked at some of the symptoms of decreased faith. It may well be that some figures in religion think increasing numbers of followers are losing faith when perhaps they are just discovering the limitations of religion and the need to separate their faith from the warped belief systems they sometimes find around them. Faith is a gift of God, religion must foster that gift and never substitute human beliefs and practices for the challenges of authentic faith. At times as we claim to search for truth we are actually hiding from it and substituting belief systems that get us nowhere.

Faith is a growing awareness or an awakening to God's love for us and within us. Faith is a gift and a self-actualization at the same time. We commit ourselves to a life based on faith; our lives are different because we appreciate God's love for us. This response to God's love in faith is itself a gift of God's love. We struggle with religion's failures and search for reasons to believe. In this search we hear the psalmist telling us, "Be strong, let your heart take courage, all who hope in the Lord" (Ps 31:24).

Having looked at some of the problems in Part I, we turn in the second part of this book to look at some of the wonderful experiences we have that point us to God, deepen our faith, and give us hope. Every day we gain glimpses of God's grace all around us. It is thrilling to appreciate the presence of God in so many aspects of each day, in wonderful things we see in ourselves, in other people who we treasure as blessings of God to us, and in the undeniable wonders of creation. We will consider the importance of the hope we find within us. This hope reveals who we are and forms the basis for our faith. It makes us open our hearts to the promises of God and challenges us to live in light of the future.

We will also consider how others help us in our discovery of faith. Community life, reconciliation, and shared prayer and worship all support and strengthen our faith. Our spiritual journey in faith and to deeper faith opens to us a profound and intimate knowledge of God. It will be a journey through darkness to greater light and illumination that will present us with new ways of experiencing faith in God's love. The love we encounter in faith is a transforming power within us, freeing us from false values and giving meaning to our lives. Let us celebrate some of the many reasons for deepening our faith.

This second part will demand more reflection of readers. We must think seriously about reasons for faith and make these reasons our own. In a world that easily disdains lives of faith, we must identify and savor these experiences that convince us of the need to build our lives on faith. Certainly not everyone will identify with all these partial experiences, and I am not suggesting they will. Living one's faith today is not filled with comforting developments. However, what I am suggesting in this Part II is that there are reasons for hope, signs of a presence that we cannot neglect, times when we are immersed in something beyond us. These experiences give justification for faith.

Chapter Six

GAINING GLIMPSES OF GRACE

Experiencing God's presence

"My soul thirsts for God, for the living God" (Ps 42:1)

There are moments in our busy lives when circumstances force us to pause and think. Maybe we caught a glimpse of a life beyond this one with its everyday interests and commitment. Perhaps we thought, felt, or experienced that this world's understanding and explanations are insufficient for growth and challenge. Maybe the only satisfactory explanation for many unusual experiences comes with awareness that there is a realm of life beyond this one that gives meaning to this one.

It could be that we are trained in scientific approaches to our world, understand and accept evolution as an obvious part of human development, and appreciate the gifts and insights scientists have brought to our understanding of our world. At the same time science does not seem to capture the whole picture, evolution does not give a complete explanation of our deeper experiences, and random development seems so inadequate an explanation for the richness of our world. At times we are shocked by what we see or experience. Is it too much to say we are surrounded by miracles, great and small, every day in our world, in other people, in our own bodies and minds, in creation around us? There are so many times when we experience a presence in our lives and in our world that is beyond normal explanation, inexplicable, and quite awesome to us. There are also times when in spite of our weaknesses, many failures, and sinful approaches to life, we are amazed at our own lives—we seem destined for more than the immediately satisfying. But there is more; we are so often shocked by others' goodness and find they are blessings to us and to the world, and it is hard to see why they should be. Finally, we live in a world of such extraordinary richness, beauty, healing, and nurturing aspects; creation calls us beyond itself to a vision of gift and of goodness that challenges us to think about our smallness, insignificance, and neediness.

So often we catch glimpses of a realm of life beyond this one that upon reflection gives meaning to this one, and we long to build bridges between these two. None of these experiences will prove the existence of God for everyone; any more than exclusively scientific explanations can prove the opposite. We are dealing with reasons or experiences that foster or strengthen faith—those original encounters of the love of God that impacted and transformed us and the way we live. It is not that we believe we encountered a life beyond this one or someone beyond this life, we know we did! It is not a belief but a vital experience, a special presence. Beliefs follow the experience of faith. Genuine faith-filled experiences of God's love whether personal, through others, or in the gift of creation, are not merely believed-in components of a religious system but vital experiences. We do not merely believe in God's love, mercy, compassion, justice, and so on, we directly and personally and vitally experience God present to us, loving us, showing us compassion, treating us with justice, and so on.

It is interesting now and again to think about sadness. Leaving aside the frequent and irrelevant times when we are sad over lost occasions for our own self-satisfaction, we must still deal with times when profound sadness fills our lives. It is not a sadness about this or that, but a sadness about the most profound aspects of life—sadness at the loss of love or inability to love, or failure to be who we think we should be, failure to be a part of a world that cannot focus on meaningful interventions, and failure of faith-filled people to make any significant impact on the values that the world ought to pursue. This sadness leaves us feeling empty. However, in emptiness we discover a new strength that surprises us. For people filled with faith the confronting of sadness and emptiness leads to fortitude. Emptiness is not a weakness but strength, the courageous strength to persevere in the discovery of one's purpose in life. What starts as sadness and emptiness can end in a presence of true peace and satisfaction, finding new guidance and purpose in the presence of God.

As people of faith, we should be naturally optimistic and enthusiastic about our lives, and convinced that they be full of joy. Joy, optimism, and enthusiasm are three interconnected concepts in the life of a person of faith. Because of our experience of God's love, we feel called to be vibrant, cheerful, full of interests, and excited about life. We find joy and happiness in making a difference to our own and to other people's lives and in giving ourselves to the appreciation of values beyond the normal horizons of life. We should enjoy doing good, being good, and experiencing ultimate goodness. We find joy and delight in the ordinary events of life. We can be fully present to people and to events, appreciating them and enjoying them as gifts that they are to us from a gracious God. Our faith gives us a new perspective on life, calling us to be present to others on a new way. Sharing is more important to us than competition with others. We can delight in others' achievements rather than comparing them to our own. A positive outlook with optimism and enthusiasm brings about joy. People of faith should enjoy life, and find this call comes from a loving and merciful God who inspires these qualities as part of faith.

When we are filled with joy we are also peacemakers, and that is one of the reasons why this energy of the spirit is so important. In a world of hatred, polarization, discrimination, and deliberate hurt, we, as people energized by joy, can bring about peacefulness in ourselves, in others around us, and in that part of society we can influence. Having stretched beyond the normal horizons of life we encounter a vision of the human community living in love and peace, and we now daily strive to make that hope a reality. So much of our experience is of a joyless world, but we sense that we have a mission to spread joy. We catch a glimpse of a joy-filled world of God's design and celebrate God's presence among us.

Being amazed at our own lives

"I am sure that he who began a good work in you will bring it to completion at the day of Jesus Christ" (Phil 1:6)

We gain glimpses of grace in our own lives. Some of the most awesome experiences we have in life are about ourselves. We become shocked to discover new insights into ourselves and our place in this world and in the realm of life beyond this one. We often find we are capable of more and better than we ever thought, and this surprises us. It is true that at times we experience dependence and insufficiency and then long for wholeness and healing. However, we discover we cannot earn these by our own efforts. Rather, as we enjoy quiet times and silence in calmness and peace, we realize our dependence and insufficiency are complemented by a power beyond us, and the wholeness and healing we seek are entirely gifts that we passively receive. In both experiences we realize that it is in receptivity that enrichment comes. We then ask ourselves from where, or from whom, does it come.

Our lives so often evidence pain in rejection and loss. We can reply in insecurity and anger but sometimes we also sense that these and other negative experiences purify and transform us. They illuminate aspects of our lives that we need to change. They give us insight into our true selves and our authentic purpose in life. At times it seems someone is compassionately guiding us through the ups and downs of life, correcting our failures, and redirecting our selfishness. In this sense of presence we gain further glimpses of grace.

It is interesting to see how deeply we feel shocked and even personally offended by injustices in our world. Part of our response is due to education and training, and certainly to conscience formation. However, we respond with a depth of emotion based upon values that relate to the nature of humanity as determined by another realm of life. We increasingly see similar reactions when faced not only with what is unjust, unfair, and inhumane, but when we must face the awful superficiality of our world and its people. We feel appalled by what we see, shocked at the emptiness and meaninglessness of what many contemporaries consider worth spending their time on. What are the criteria for making these judgments of what is inadequately human and why do we feel ashamed at having failed our Creator?

At other times we are amazed at our own reflections on life and people and wonder where did we get these ideas. Sometimes we evidence convictions and do not know how we got them. We see ourselves, family, and friends sharing brilliant intuitions and appreciate that we and they manifest realities beyond our and their capabilities. Some of these awesome experiences remain unexplained outside the enriching gifts that are intimate parts of an experience of faith. These snapshots point to a higher level of life that seems to be ours.

Part of our daily lives is to know who we are, why we are here, how we should relate to others, what it means to be human, and is there any reason for our existence in this world. When we sense someone saying "you are mine" as happens to people of faith who listen to God's call, then our lives take on a deeper meaning. Men and women of faith seek meaning and understanding of the beginning and end of life. We deal with an inner longing of our soul, a yearning for fulfillment. We conclude this world is an insufficient explanation of who we are, and that an adequate understanding must come from somewhere else. At times we sense a personal purpose in life and identify it as a calling to become who we were created and destined to be.

One of the delightful and ever surprising experiences that amaze us and challenge us to think about faith and to become aware of glimpses into its source is the experience of love. Whether we discover our love for someone or discover that we are loved by someone, either case draws new levels of awareness and understanding of ourselves and others in community. When we find we selflessly and unconditionally love, or we find that we are loved selflessly and unconditionally, it gives rise to a new appreciation of ourselves. Loving, and being loved, finding we and others are loveable changes our approach to life, to oneself, and to others. Then we see in so many experiences that we are loved by a greater force outside of ourselves. Sometimes, we see and feel moments and experiences of inexplicable love that fill us with a joy beyond this world. Although living in a world of hatred, we sense we were created for love and, upon reflection, by Love.

Witnessing that others are blessings to us

"In humility count others better than yourselves" (Phil 2:3)

We gain many glimpses of grace, signs of divine presence, in the actions and reactions we witness in the lives of good people. Our world is for the most part not a pleasant place to live in. Crime is everywhere, incompetence and corruption are more common in government than their absence, greed is the common characteristic of business, and war is the preferred answer from the fools in national and international government. We must live with bigotry, violence, racism, and hate. We all get used to expecting the worst from organizations and individuals, and we live in fear. However, in the midst of all of this we hear constant stories of heroism, self-sacrifice, people dying to save others, activists who will not give up, and so many who have suffered horrendously and bounce back with resiliency and forgiveness. There seems to be something deep in people's hearts that enables them to be models of goodness in the midst of evil, and we are inspired and called by their goodness to think of values beyond our confining world.

It is easier when we think of family, friends, and nurturing communities, where we feel supported, loved, and also challenged. We look at those around us and see them as blessings to us and to the world. Sometimes we pause to think of how wonderful a spouse is, how delightful to be with grandchildren and appreciate in awe and wonder their growth and development. We see how wonderful it is to share joy with family and friends, and how self-sacrificing parents can be, and how peaceful and enriching the elderly can be. We know we are witnessing something beyond normal, and through other people's extraordinariness we receive a touch of God's love and goodness.

Now and again, we meet a person whose very lifestyle impresses us profoundly and calls us to think about ultimate values. It may be a man or woman whose personal integrity makes them stand out as models of wholeness in a frequently corrupt world. Sometimes we meet a person who seems too innocent for this world but who calls us to the values God places before each of us. We all know someone who is either very rich or very poor, but whose whole life focuses on generosity and reminds us of the selflessness, goodness, and generosity of God. In spite of sinful wars all around us, we witness individuals and organizations that give their lives to strive for peace and become the peacemakers that Jesus hoped would point others to God. Again, many people give us insights into ultimate goodness in the way they dedicate their lives to giving, receiving, modeling, and teaching compassion.

Good men and women, often in the hardest circumstances become prophets, calling the world's communities to become aware that something is wrong in our values. They call us to weep at crime, violence, and degrading brutality. They never let us hide from the failures and inhumanity of so-called civilized countries and their proxy wars, destruction of the innocent, and the murdering and marauding armies of wealthy nations. We need these prophets to denounce injustice and challenge us to a vision of hope.

A quality we often find in others and that in a particular way reflects the God of our faith encounter in love is when people work to bring the best out of others. Men and women who work in service, or are teachers, healthcare providers, counselors, religious ministers, first responders, and so on, all these show a concern for others and a dedication to their betterment. However, now and again we meet people who go beyond their professional commitment to a new level of discretionary commitment that is way beyond what is professionally required in their daily service. Such people reach levels of self-sacrifice and service of others that are truly remarkable and call to our minds and hearts the words of Jesus, "No one has greater love than this, to lay down one's life for one's friends" (Jn 15:13). This is a daily occurrence in our troubled world and these people call us to think of values that can transform us.

Every society has found space for individuals to give themselves to the pursuit of life with God. Their dedication, asceticism, and prayer help them to stand out in our midst as signs pointing to transcendent values and reminding us of the transitoriness of this world and our lives. These monks, ascetics, and other dedicated men and women, give testimony to their authentic encounter with transcendent life and with that realm of life beyond this one. Moreover, along with these ascetics we also recognize mystics and saints whose lives of prayer and contemplation teach us how to journey to God.

Enjoying the wonders of creation

"Ever since the creation of the world his invisible nature . . .
has been clearly perceived in things that have been made"
(Rom 1:20)

At one time or another we are all struck by the beauty of creation. We love the beauty of God's creation not just in general but particular occasions constantly arise when we are struck by the richness, beauty, and overwhelming diversity of creation. The world of God's creation and of human development has generally been viewed as one of the three great enemies of a person's spiritual growth, and so ascetics fled the world because they saw that men and women can become enslaved to the world's values and instead of possessing the world become possessed by it. However, creatures, in spite of their beauty, cannot become ends in themselves. It is not that we are opposed to nature, but we know it can become a block to union with God when people are attached and possessive of things. It is also true that there is frequently violence in creation and destruction in its cycles. So, people of faith actively participate in a purification process whereby enjoyment of creation is never an end in itself.

As we journey to God along the spiritual path, we find a new freedom in dealing with the world and see it as God's gift. This is the development of the journey and life of love that makes things different and enables us to look at the world in a different way. People filled with faith and the love it brings look at the world around them differently, and suddenly the whole world speaks of the presence of God and offers glimpses of God's love. Moreover, we discover that during the spiritual journey creation can lead us to God. We find creation is a hidden presence of God. This is important for it helps us appreciate the greatness of God's love and generosity in creation and can thus awaken our love of God who alone is able to create this diversity and grandeur. When we look at the world in this way we discover we are surrounded by many signs of God's presence. We see God's wisdom and judgment in the wonders around us.

Furthermore, in our approach to creation, especially in times of prayerful reflection all creation is transformed and becomes part of our vision of God. This is a glimpse into the inner world of God's love, and we begin to see that world differently and sense something of its beauty and wonder. Earlier in the spiritual journey, creation is a reflection of God's beauty, and when we look at the world it reveals something of God's generous love. Later reflection moves us to appreciate how all created things are integral to God's vision of love. Creation no longer simply reveals God to us but it is a sacramental presence of God.

So, we gradually move from renunciation to seeing reflections of God's beauty in creation, to an appreciation of the sacramental quality of creation, and finally move on to a wonderful conclusion; that a person knows creatures through God and not God through creatures. At this time a person experiences an awakening of the Word in the deepest part of his or her spirit, so that all creation seems to move in unison, and manifests its beauty, power, loveliness, and graces. Then we become conscious of how all creatures, earthly and heavenly, have their life, duration, and strength in God.

We are led to an extraordinary conclusion, namely, that a person now knows all these created things better in God than in themselves. This is a reversal of our normal ways of thinking about these things: we know the effects through the cause and not the cause through the effects. This is a new supernatural vision of the relationship between God and creation. This is a mystical vision of the cosmos, in which every creature has its place and meaning in the plan of God, for all creation is restored in God's transforming love. This gives us an appreciation of the whole world as sharing in the glory of God, and the love we now find in the world is the epiphany of God's love. When we look at the world we are convinced there is love behind it. For many people the beauty around them challenges them to believe in a power beyond this world, but unfortunately they resist the consequences of their convictions and even participate in the destruction of our world.

We live surrounded by the blessings of God; small and great miracles of God's love in our midst. We can easily take these wondrous gifts for granted instead of allowing them to remind us of the life of faith to which we are called. If we reflect on our daily lives and see the treasures of goodness all around us, we must inevitably think of God in whom we gratefully place our faith.

Personal reflection

Every day is an exciting experience of God's constant nudges to faith. I feel surrounded by multiple signs of God's loving presence. I am reminded of an old English hymn that tells us "the whole world is full of the presence of God, but only they who see take off their shoes." I can find no other explanation for these miracles all around us except that they are gifts of a loving God.

Questions for discussion or personal reflection

1. How does the world around you speak to you about God?

2. Give a few examples of glimpses of grace that you have noticed.

3. Why do you described yourself as a believer?

Chapter Seven
LIVING IN HOPE

Hope reveals who we are

*"Always be prepared to make a defense . . . for the hope
that is in you" (1 Pet 3:15)*

One of the greatest reasons we find to believe is the awareness deep within our inner spirits of a hope that cannot be denied.[9] Hope is our conviction of what the future will be like and should be like. It implies a dynamic commitment, a passionate pursuit of the better future that is foreseen, and so hope is never passive. For a person of faith, hope is a way of looking at reality, a kind of perception, an insight into possibilities, and an understanding of what will happen. Hope is not a dream, but it is the basic attitude that makes all dreams possible. When we become aware of ourselves as incomplete human beings, open to betterment, and called to fulfillment, then immediately we are filled with hope. Hope is about the meaning of life, about what it means to be human. It is the foundation of a desire for transformation, the awareness that things will be different than they are. For each of us, hope is the conviction that we are being drawn to a new and greater reality.

The past is never decisive for a great present, the future is. The unborn future may lie in the past, and we can anticipate a fulfilled past in the future, but it is always hope that gives a meaningful expression to life in the present. Hope is greater than the accumulation of memories, for no matter how great they are the reality they represented has gone. The past may be prologue, but a person inspired by a faith-filled experience of God looks with conviction to the future. It always implies resiliency and openness, for hope-filled visions evolve, and we must struggle to fulfill them. However, the object of hope is not yet present to us and so cannot be the object of confidence. Rather, hope can be transformed into reality, even when hope seems beyond reason, when we are convinced of the future in faith.

I believe that hope is a forgotten virtue, a discarded energy of the human spirit, and a lost dimension of life. However, we perceive that hope is critical to human development, for when we have no hope everything falls apart, every other virtue and quality suffers. Without hope people are paralyzed, and they live in the hell of hopelessness, as Dante suggested when above the gates of hell he placed the sign, "Abandon hope, all you who enter here" (Inferno, Canto III). The future for which we hope gives meaning to all present reality. Hope is the greatest motivator of human development for we live in so far as we have hope.

We instinctively hope. It is part of human nature to yearn, to search for fullness of life, to create a future about which people can be enthusiastic. It is part of human existence to hope, and men and women discover and realize their hopes in interaction with the world. However, our daily efforts never seem to realize all that we yearn for. We all understand that we carry within us the desire to be who are capable of being, and we must never neglect these yearnings of hope. But the hope inspired by faith is more than this.

We place our faith in what we hope for

"Now faith is the assurance of things hoped for, the conviction of things not seen" (Heb 11:1).

Hope is the most basic attitude of Christian faith. A person has faith in what he or she hopes for. Hope is rooted in faith and is the proof of belief. Hope is a way of life. We do not accept ourselves, other people, organizations, or situations, as they are, but see what they can become and courageously and perseveringly make decisions in light of what we hope for. Heraclitus pointed out, "He who does not hope for what is beyond expectation will not find it."

Hope, in so far as it is the concrete expression of faith, cannot be reduced to expectations, or to what is merely realizable or possible, or even to an unenlightened utopia. Moreover, the hope of faith is not the accumulation of easily attained individual hopes or what we yearn for when we are at our best. We are not talking about people who hope for this or for that. The hoped-for vision that determines how we live in the present is the vision of life with God that we learn in faith. This is the reality behind what we believe that challenges the way we live in the present. "Now hope that is seen is not hope. For who hopes for what is seen? But if we hope for what we do not see, we wait for it with patience" (Rom 8:24-25). For Christians, Jesus' resurrection to new life is an affirmation of the future and a passage to a new hope that changes the way we live in the present.

The object of hope implies knowledge, for it is not guesswork or the arrival of the unexpected. It includes a commitment to community, for it is not solitary or isolationist. It stresses an appreciation of history, especially salvation history, for it is the hope of humanity not of some individual. It includes awareness of sin and human weakness, for it is not a utopian ideal. It focuses on ultimate hope in union with God in freedom from everlasting death, for it is not the good but minor hopes of each day. It is a gift of God to faith-filled dedication, for it is not something men and women can attain by themselves. Hope does not give us peace and satisfaction, but it causes unrest, impatience, restlessness, and dissatisfaction, as we face ourselves, others, and a world in need of transformation. We cannot reconcile ourselves with what we see, but only with what we hope will be achieved as part of the vision of God that we experience in an encounter of faith.

So, while faith gives rise to hope, hope is God's gift to men and women, and the language of religion is generally the language of hope, for it speaks of newness of life for individuals and redemptive liberation for the whole of creation. Hope gives us glimpses beyond the normal horizons of life into an afterlife that conditions how we live in this one. As a result of this insight into the horizons of hope, our transcendental hope challenges us to make ourselves into who we are capable of being through daily decisions and choices. We realize our hope for the vision of God in daily activity, and the daily future we create makes the ultimate future a reality, as we live it and grow into it through patience and fortitude.

Having given ourselves to God in faith, we begin with a spiritual journey into the depths of our hearts and inner convictions, where alone, we hear a call that no one else hears. This call is first of all to transform ourselves and our role in the world and then to reach out to contribute to the transformation of others, individually and in society. It is common to speak about our inner spirit and motivation, but our primary motivating attitude is hope. There is no faith without self-transformation. We develop life based on core values, but these values are part of the vision of hope. Hope is not a skill set, although it will require new skills. Hope is our inner motivation, the fundamental modifier of life. Everything else can be a technique, including faith (when it is generally interpreted as a belief system) and even love. Hope cannot be a technique, although talking about hope can be, as we have seen in several political figures and processes.

Hope reflects the true inner convictions of a person. It results from conversion and is proof of faith. Individuals and organizations that look to the past or extrapolate from the present are destined to fail, whereas the great person of faith looks to the future in hope, dedicates self to moral renewal, focuses on the essential human values contained in the orientation of hope, and motivates and mobilizes others to attain the new vision of hope. For such a person hope is the source of life and the greatest reason for faith.

Hope opens our hearts to a God of promise

> *"May the God of hope fill you with all joy and peace in believing, so that you may abound in hope by the power of the Holy Spirit" (Rom 15:13)*

What people believe in they hope for. If they did not hope for the object of their faith, then the latter would be empty words.

We believe that at the end of this age we will participate in the age to come. So it is that Christianity for sure, and other religions too, speak of the Promised Land, the kingdom that will come, the future reign of God, a new creation, the universal resurrection, forgiveness, and redemption. "By awesome deeds you answer us with deliverance, O God of our salvation; you are the hope of all the ends of the earth and of the farthest seas" (Ps 65:5). These are the components of hope, and we cling to this hope because God is a God of promise; not an empty promise but one we are convinced will be real.

"The Lord is my portion, says my soul, therefore I will hope in (God)" (Lam 3:24). Hope is a moral virtue that implies obligations on the person of faith who must live in light of the hope in which he or she claims to believe. Hope is a charism in some individuals, enabling them to motivate others with their enthusiasm for what can lie ahead. Hope is also a spiritual energy that moves individuals to involve the whole self in attaining the goals of hope. When these various aspects of hope come together the end transforms every day.

The problem of spirituality and human activity in the present world depends on how we see the relationship between the human spirit and the absolute end in God. The fact that God is a God of promise means the faithful lovingly commit themselves to live in "the hope of righteousness" (Gal 5:5). Moreover, the end we see in hope is not just the transformation of humanity but also the reconciliation of societies, and the liberation and harmony of all creation. In other words, our hope is that the whole of reality will be healed and brought into union. This vision is the promise of God, the object of our hope, and the sphere of our spiritual commitment. "Hope does not disappoint us, because God's love has been poured into our hearts through the Holy Spirit that has been given to us" (Rom 5:5). The awesome and overwhelming love of God calls us to live out our lives in the presence of people, institutions, events, and creation, all longing for transformation, all already transformed in our hope.

When we think about what we believe and the hope that lies ahead in the promise of God, in other words, that our "faith and hope are set on God" (1 Pet 1:21), we discover two aspects of this vision. First, it includes the fulfillment of all that we yearn for as human beings: to live without threats to peace, free from our own inadequacies, saved from weaknesses and sin that make us less than we want to be. It finds satisfaction, pleasure and joy in life, respect and fulfillment in a meaningful life. It welcomes us as an integral part of community, sharing mutual love, and discovering the enrichment of life together. So, we want to discover we can be the best we are capable of being. Second, we hope to benefit from experiences beyond our expectations, we presume we will be surprised, we feel life will be more than we ever thought, and we hope to be transformed in union with God. Humanity is divided into two groups, those whose hopes are limited and end with the end of this world and those whose hopes are intimately linked to the vision of a world to come. We, as faith-filled people, open our hearts to a God of promise. We can never be satisfied with mediocrity, but must always pursue the excellence of hope, struggling each day to make today an anticipation of tomorrow's hopes. When we say that all authority is from God, a statement of hope, it changes the way in which men and women live each day.

Hope challenges us to live in light of the future

Let us "seize the hope set before us" (Heb 6:18)

The only real question for human beings is what will happen at the end of life. The way we view the end in hope can revolutionize how we deal with the present. In general, if we make the end time irrelevant, we make our lives meaningless and irrelevant too. I say "in general" for we have all met good moral atheists whose lives are filled with goodness and who put believers to shame. For people of faith, hoping in God's promise is a belief in God's involvement in development and history. "For surely I know the plans I have for you, says the Lord, plans for your welfare and not for harm, to give you a future with hope" (Jer 29:11). Hope has become this-worldly. If we know what we hope for, we will be dissatisfied with society, its structures, and its relationships. Our hope is a judgment on the failure and inadequacies of the past, the present, and the future without God. We look to the future with conviction, and in the promise of God we see a vision of justice, community, and mutuality in relationships.

Faith means being committed to hope. Hope becomes a way of approaching the present because of what we believe in the future. We live in spiritual tension between "the already" and "the not yet." "So, if anyone is in Christ, there is a new creation; everything old has passed away; see, everything has become new!" (2 Cor 5:17). So, our hope demands that we live responsibly in the modern world. Nowadays, hope for the promises of God in afterlife has become hope for the world as an anticipation of the afterlife. Put another way, hope should make us creative in dealing with the present and challenge us to create a desirable future in the present, not just for ourselves but for others too, for hope is always a shared hope. Hope is a way of living one's faith and love. What is "there and then" inspires us to develop a "here and now."

Frequently, we see thought of the afterlife as a distraction from involvement in the present. However, the way we dedicate ourselves to the transformation of the present is more determined by how we view the afterlife than by anything else. Hope for the future does not despise the "now" of the present. Rather, it sees now as part of the hoped-for future, a step on the way. Living in hope is the best way to give fullness to the present moment, for genuine hope is optimism filled with realism.

So, the future becomes real in our lives as hope-filled people who see present dedication as a participation in the truth of the future. However, this hope is never merely individual, for the object of hope is communal; God's promise is for the whole human community. So, men and women work together to attain their hope, each person looking to others as integral to his or her own development. Hope gives rise to the duty to peace, justice, and human development. Individuals may have competing small hopes. But the hoped-for future is a shared, common hope for which we work together in love. We work together to implement hope. We may well start with all the small hopes of each day but the true believer's hope is a part of a vision of life, a philosophy of life, a way of approaching life.

Hope gives meaning to the present and challenges us to live in light of the future. In fact, hope is intimately connected with death and calls us to make decisions in the context of our own deaths. In such a vision hope means bringing out the best in ourselves and in every person with whom we work and in every part of an organization with which we interact. Changing the present to reflect the future is the task of people who understand their interconnectedness with everyone else. As people of hope, grounded in a vision of the future, we find challenge, direction, common identity, and connections that lead to common hope, spiritual renewal, and unending challenge. Nothing brings greater clarity to life than death. Peter in his first letter tells us we must always be ready to give an account of the hope that lies within us. He points out that there is a difference between the hope and the account. The latter is not the hope itself. We must defend our hope, and we do that by the life that we live individually and in organizations.

As people of confident hope we can respond with humility and become servants of a shared hope, giving to others reasons for living and reasons for hoping amidst the pressures of modern life. "Always be ready to make your defense to anyone who demands from you an accounting for the hope that is in you" (1 Pet 3:15). The vision of hope reflects the basic elements for a program of action we can pursue. "Let us hold fast to the confession of our hope without wavering, for (God) who has promised is faithful" (Heb 10:23). This is God's vision for the welfare of humanity; a program of action for human beings in their personal and institutional renewal. So, hope is the basis of faith and motivates us in the strengthening of our life of faith.

So, hope reveals the greater truth of each of us and what we really believe. It explains the ultimate meaning of life and therefore informs how we deal with the present. When we understand this we can motivate others to greatness. Our faith is based on what we hope for in personal transformation in this world and union with the Lord in the next. Let our reflections on hope strengthen our faith.

Personal reflection

When we struggle with the challenges of faith, we can become discouraged and depressed—I know I do. Only hope keeps us going; it sustains and nourishes our faith. It is not that we hope the Church will change; that would require a lot of conversions and there is no sign that is going to happen. Rather, our hope is in God, the heart of our faith. We know there can be no hope without adversity. But filled with faith, we must walk through "the door of hope" (Hos 2:15) for "we are prisoners of hope" (Zech 9:12)

Questions for discussion or personal reflection

1. Why is it important that we live in hope?

2. Have you thought about what happens at death? How do you prepare yourself?

3. What do you hope for and who can fulfill your hopes?

Chapter Eight

JOURNEYING WITH OTHERS IN DISCOVERING FAITH

Discovering God in community

"Love one another as I have loved you" (Jn 15:12)

When we have a faith-filled experience of God's love we see that the purpose of creation is the expansion of love—that the love of God for God passes through us and returns to God. This is love's vision, and our part in this vision is to build loving communities at all levels of our lives. So, early Christians clearly understood that authentic conversion included the acceptance of a community dimension to their new life. This emphasis on community today is not meant to be a denial of, or in opposition to, our spiritual development as individuals, but it does indicate our conviction that to be dedicated to community is the finest way to affirm and live out the best in ourselves. But what is it about community that gives us reasons for faith?

We discover that community is the way of life to which God calls us, and it focuses us on what Jesus hopes will become the community's greatest testimony: love. Jesus said it would prove to the world that we are his disciples. The vision Jesus offers us is one of universal unity— a life of union that prepares us for union with God. It is a vision beyond our normal daily lives; it is a vision of the ultimate meaning of life. It is a concrete expression of our faith in God's love. So, unless we Christians exist as a community, we do not exist as an authentic manifestation of Jesus' followers to the world. Thus, the vocation and mission of the Christian community is to be a dynamic sacrament of communion: an outward sign to the world of God's grace. We are greater in community than we are as separate parts. When we see this move from self-centeredness to self-transcendence we ask why do we do this, and it points to a world beyond this one. We discover we are incomplete without others— not just groups or crowds, but people of like-mind, like-heart, and similar values. We ask ourselves why we center out lives on others and not on ourselves. This awareness strengthens our faith.

The communal nature and mission of Christian discipleship respond to the deep needs of all men and women who yearn for freedom from loneliness, from alienation from society, from personal isolation, and from a sense of rootlessness and anonymity. The fact that no one can achieve his or her destiny in isolation but only in and with others is a driving force that brings humanity together and leads all people to a dynamic interrelationship which facilitates a deeper appreciation of our shared faith. We discover a new level of awareness that we exist for each other. Faith assures us that community is a more authentic expression of human life because we are made in the image of God. Moreover, we often find that other people prepare the way for faith.

Trying to be with others in the way of love, however, quickly makes us understand we can only exist together as God's own family.

No one can make it on his or her own but only as part of a people who worship God in love. Our faith convinces us that the way of love is communal, that loving others as we journey to God is not just an option, it is an integral element of the journey, a reflection of God's life of Trinitarian love. In this way, we appreciate our place in salvation history and in the communion of saints.

One of the great advantages of community in relation to faith is that together we can discern essentials of faith and beliefs, sharing not only love but also common values and vision. In fact, our communities when dedicated to genuine values and not to so many secondary issues that often clutter faith, can become standards of faith for us all. Communities uphold members in faith, strengthen each other, and can become a powerful prophetical presence and challenge for faith.

Communities help each other to become God's presence to the world, which was exactly what Jesus hoped would happen. To do this, they must together achieve four steps—root, interpret, implement, and discover. First, they must assure each other that the values of faith and belief that they live and proclaim can be genuinely rooted in Jesus' teaching and are not inauthentic add-ons that religions are always tempted to look to. Second, they cannot remain back in Jesus' time as some fundamentalist religious traditions do. It is one thing to root beliefs in Jesus but that only tells us what discipleship was over two thousand years ago. So, there must be continuity between a contemporary form of Christianity and its roots. We must interpret these teachings and beliefs for our own times and thus make them relevant for today. Then, third, these interpreted beliefs must be implemented or incarnated in our everyday life with its cultural differences. It is here where interpreted beliefs are different in presentation in order to be the same in essence; they must change in order to remain the same. Fourth, beliefs must be ever relevant to changing circumstances, cultures, and peoples, and so faith-filled people must be on the look-out to discover new ways of living faith, new beliefs to concretize faith, new vitality so that faith in a loving God is ever present in changing times.[10]

Finding God in reconciliation

> *"So if you are offering your gift at the altar, and there remember your brother has something against you, leave your gift there before the altar and go; first be reconciled to your brother, and then come and offer your gift" (Mt 5:23-24)*

There is an intimate connection between our individual growth in faith and love and our growth as communities of love. Yet we often face a rather dusty road in the practice of building loving communities, and we sometimes even end up with "communities" in which people are isolated and anonymous. While it is true that early Christians were known for their community, fellowship, and love, it is not true for many of us Christians today. In fact, the work of God's love within us is threatened by our lack of reconciliation with one another. Certainly there seems at times more divisiveness than love in us. The strangest thing is that so much of our animosity is over non-essential issues. If we focus on the essentials of faith, we can find mutual support and strength.

Our commitment to reconciliation both strengthens and manifests our faith. Life in the contemporary Church is increasingly a call to reconciliation, which is precisely how Paul viewed the needs of the early Church. He told the rather divisive Corinthian community: "Everything has become new! All this is from God, who reconciled us to himself through Christ, who has given us the ministry of reconciliation; that is, in Christ God was reconciling the world to himself" (2 Cor 5:18-19). Everyone who wishes to walk along the way of love must both model reconciliation and proclaim it, aware that unless we exist as a reconciling community we cannot exist as Christians at all, and we lose our potential for individual spiritual growth. This calls us to rekindle our enthusiasm to search and work for a vision of unity and to rededicate ourselves to acquire skills of communication, community building, understanding, conflict management, and the art of healing divisions and mutual distrust, fostering dialogue, and challenging discrimination. Faith calls us to wholeness as a people and we ask ourselves why we are drawn together in faith and love.

Nothing takes precedence over reconciliation, not even the outward worship of God (see Mt 5:23-24). Reconciliation is linked to our humanness and wholeness, and when absent our worship is nothing but empty words. Reconciliation needs honesty, faith, prayer, and the grace of the Lord. It takes two, for it is a total gift of self, total reception of others, and total sharing. It is manifested in forgiveness and produces a communion of peace that prophetically challenges the world to believe. When reconciliation is lost, the community loses its value and meaning; and when we refuse to be reconciled, we destroy the Christian dimension of our own personality. We find faith includes forgiveness which would be meaningless without our experience of God's love. We have witnessed many lost opportunities for reconciliation in our contemporary politics, social life, family life, and Church life. We remind ourselves that reconciliation helps us discover our common faith; it is a reason to believe.

Every act of reconciliation is liberating and creative, because it is a sharing in the divine life of love. Paul claimed that the whole message of salvation could be summed up in the idea of reconciliation: "In Christ God was reconciling the world to himself

. . . and entrusting the message of reconciliation to us" (2 Cor 5:19). This relationship between reconciliation and Christian faith is so intimate that we must recommit ourselves to dialogue that leads to reconciliation. Every situation we deal with in community, including conflict and opposition, can become an opportunity for resurrection, and we grow through such situations as we journey together to greater faith-filled love. The challenge to proclaim reconciliation within contemporary Church communities starts by reaching out to those the Church has marginalized or rejected. It means building bridges to people who are more conservative or liberal than we consider ourselves to be. It means listening to what young people have to say. All these voices can challenge and strengthen faith.

At the local level of Church life, whatever the composition of the group, there are several attitudes that lead toward a reconciling community. First of all we need mutual respect and benevolence towards one another—something so often lacking in our encounters today. Aware that religion is a mystery with few definitive answers, we have to try to understand others' different views and enter into dialogue with them to enrich our own perspective—not to convince others that we are right and they are wrong. This approach should be accompanied by constant self-questioning. It used to go without saying, but recent experience has reminded us that we need to urge believers of all persuasions to avoid deliberate attempts to find fault with others and to follow Christian teaching regarding freedom of conscience. This is part of self-correction and ongoing conversion. We journey with others to discover faith.

Christian redemptive love requires risk taking, care for each other, supportiveness, compassion without pity, and love without sentimentality. Maintaining reconciling love is especially difficult in times of transition, when we must enter the suffering of others and work together for a better vision of a loving community that liberates all humans from whatever burdens they endure. Living in a reconciling community gives us confidence in our shared faith. When we see reconciling love, we know there lies something beyond the present—a goal of God's love to be pursued together.

Worshipping God in community

"My real life is the faith I have in the Son of God, who loved me, and gave himself for me" (Gal 2:20)

Our lives of faith are lived out each day in family, work, social development, and local Church activities. However, life's ordinariness and God's awesomeness come together in personal prayer and celebrational worship—both of which show forth our faith. After all, the prime responsibility of people of faith is to celebrate individually and communally their love and dedication to God. But the attitudes necessary for prayer and liturgy grow out of the ordinary interactions of each day. In prayer we open ourselves to the action of the Spirit within us and actualize aspects of our personalities otherwise never seen. It is principally in prayer that we live as true children of God, become aware that we are part of God's family, and are challenged to live as community. In prayer and worship we become aware that the Holy Spirit is active within us and that our faith is nurtured by God—wonderful confirmations of our experience of faith.

Prayer and worship underline our purpose in life, give reasons for the way we ought to live, and reinforce a sense of community and shared values. Prayer and worship remind us that we are on pilgrimage, that we find our own fulfillment in God alone, and that we were created to discover and embrace God's love. In prayer and worship we appreciate how others respond in faith to God's love, with them we feel called to action to show faith, and above all we discover openings to the inner world of God's presence. Prayer and worship give new meaning to our lives, articulate our faith, and present us with a second horizon of life.

Prayer requires quiet time and calmness in which we can spend time away from the clutter of life and oppose its superficiality and endless distractions. It is a time when we can think about important things, try to put life in perspective, and embrace our reasons for existence. Prayer is a time to prepare our bodies and our hearts to be receptive. We first focus on ourselves in order to focus outside of ourselves. We center our entire beings on seeking God. This requires stillness of body, inspiration by the Spirit, concentration with Christ and silence in God. These four remote preparations help us to be receptive to life beyond us and find our faith confirmed.

Being present to God in prayer gradually means letting go of former ways of knowing and loving God and opening our hearts to new experiences. This is a time of simplification of prayer and of the laying aside of prayer structures and methods that we once controlled so well. Prayer gradually consists of few words, few thoughts; it is more a loving attention to God. Put briefly, this stage means talking less and loving more.

Our final way of relating to God in prayer is to be open to receive. We have learnt that our contribution amounts to removing obstacles of a false self, an inaccurate understanding of prayer, and a too-human perception of God. Our primary response is openness and receptivity, letting God transform us in every aspect of our being. The strategy of giving time to reflection and prayer is a decision for depth, enrichment, and transformation in our spiritual lives. Being constantly connected to God through prayer helps empty us of selfishness, brings us the power to be our true selves, and lets us live out our faith.

When prayer is a community expression of faith, it becomes a reliving of the mysteries of Christ's love within the liturgical year or in the Eucharist. These great events grow out of daily life. As we distance ourselves from the inadequacies of our world we find how much we long for God and for answers to the meaning of life. This God-centered search becomes full of a sense of awe and mystery. These personal reactions are complemented by community awareness and acknowledgment of God's interventions in our lives. Liturgy is an interruption of life to refocus on major priorities of human existence. It shocks us into an awareness that our lives are a small part of something great. We relive what we originally experienced in a faith-filled encounter with God.

Christian faith means centering one's life on others. In our anonymous and selfish world, we make this great priority of Jesus our own. We must strive to build community at all levels of our life. We build community, dedicate ourselves to reconciliation with everyone, and we pray and worship together. The challenge of faith is always to move away from self-centeredness to center our lives on others and in doing so we discover that God in whom we place our faith is with us.

Personal reflection

I have to admit that I find parish activities unhelpful and a large percentage of community liturgies boring and uninspirational. But I know I cannot isolate myself in a personalized version of faith. Fortunately, my wife is my greatest inspiration, challenge, critic, and evaluator of my reflections on faith. Then I have colleagues whose dedication and views challenge and sustain me. I am also fortunate to know several priests who can lead a liturgy and preach meaningfully.

Questions for discussion or personal reflection

1. What can you do to sustain so many who long for spiritual growth in faith and cannot find it?

2. What roles do other people play in your journey of faith?

3. Do you think your local Church community is a model of the values of faith?

Chapter Nine
LIVING IN THE DARKNESS THAT ILLUMINES FAITH

The journey of faith

"For you are all sons and daughters of the light and sons and daughters of the day; we are not of the night or of darkness"
(1 Thess 5:4-5)

We have examined reasons for believing and found that we are surrounded by the wonders of God's grace, we are filled with longings of hope that can only find fulfillment in God, and we are so enriched by others in our common search for faith. Let us now look at the many reasons for faith growth that we experience in our own spiritual journey to God. This is a journey that goes through darkness to light and illumination. We see that God is with us, every step of the way, and this awareness can strengthen faith. Spirituality is a journey of faith in ourselves, in others, in the goodness of creation, in ultimate values, and in God. No journey is straight forward and smooth;

there are always ups and downs and temporary setbacks. There are frequently delays, diversions, and longer sections of the journey than expected. Sometimes, when we think we have arrived, we find it is just a junction leading to another section of the journey. We cannot grow to our full potential unless we can also accept the emptiness we experience on this journey—emptiness that only the Lord can then fill. This is what our journey of faith is all about. Spirituality is our faith brought to birth in ever-changing circumstances of modern life. Faith allows God's power to be fruitful in us.

Our spirituality grows principally when we allow God to purify, direct, and enrich our lives; we let God transform us without us placing obstacles to God's actions within us. Spirituality is rooted in a faith experience, in our case in Christ and in our common search to bring about the coming of the Kingdom he announced. This journey demands deliberate action by us based on decisions made in light of faith. The most important decisions are made when we confront the dark nights of faith. There are lots of experiences of emptiness and loss in our journey, but they help us discover the importance of receptivity and openness to God's grace within us.

The point of departure for our spiritual journey is awareness that we are born into a situation of disorder; our entire lives ought to be subordinated to the Spirit, but instead they go the other way, to sense. More men and women are guided by sense than by the Spirit, and this degrades their faith. The result of this natural decline is that we hide our own true image, dignity, and finality, tend to continually regress instead of making progress, and even block the life of faith within us. We are surrounded by disorders; but, let us be clear, we cause these disorders because we are disordered people—we lack order or direction in our spiritual lives. Faith cannot grow in these situations. We want to progress but at times we are unable to do so, in fact we even seem to be paralyzed. So, if we wish to make the journey of faith to God, where alone we will find our authentic selves, then we must be willing to undertake the rigors of this journey. The bright light of faith shines only after we endure the experience of darkness that purifies faith. After all, the journey can be hard, and spiritual life and prayer can be dry, boring, and empty. In this journey we are not alone, nor are we struggling to move forward. Rather, God takes the initiative and draws us to divine life and love.

There are two emphases, aspects, or levels to this journey of faith; at one time we may emphasize or experience one of them and at other times the other. As long as it is clear that eventually both must go together in an integrated spiritual commitment. First, we must center the journey on knowing God in faith. This is a process of interiorization and purification of our concepts of God. It is important because if we do not purify faith we remain stunted, never touch the reality of God, drag along behind us an image of God from former times, and end up seeing ourselves when we look at God. God is nothing like we think God is, and we must remove all the idols and false images of God to arrive at mature faith. So, we must eliminate all false, sensible images and all intellectual information about God that we may have valued in the past, for God is not like creatures, and most images we have are just idols. However, second, in addition to experiencing that God is not like we think God is, we also find that God does not act towards us in the ways we thought God would; God does not correspond to ideas we have of divine life. So, we will find there are two rhythms to the journey of faith; a theoretical one challenging us to purify our images of God, and a vital one in which God in contemplative prayer teaches us that God acts differently towards us than we expected.

We can never earn the right to make this journey to deeper faith; it is an invitation from a loving God. It is not easy, and some people do not want to undergo this journey of faith and its purification because their image of God is part of the comfort and consolation they find in religion and its belief systems. Sometimes we would like to encounter God but do not see God acting in our lives because our false image acts like a cataract that hinders clear vision. If we have the courage to make this spiritual journey God will correct our false understandings of faith and enrich our vision of faith. When we look back over the development of our spiritual lives we know that God was acting in us and still is.

Entering darkness and finding light

"I will turn the darkness before them into light" (Is 42:16)

Our spiritual journey takes us through periods of darkness in faith. This part of our spiritual lives is very difficult for all of us, for it means we have to learn to accept what God allows and what life brings us, while living in a world of action, ministry, community, and spiritual techniques. We must let God work in us freely without hindrance. When we look back over the history of spirituality we find that all great figures had to pass through solitude, darkness, emptiness, and the desert in order to find answers to the most profound questions of faith. Only when we have the courage to face and enter the darkness of faith can we deal with our own meaning and destiny. It is darkness that brings illumination; that thick darkness where God dwells (Ex 20:21). The thought of living, learning, and growing in darkness seems so strange to us. To be in darkness does not mean that you cannot see or that you have no vision. It is a call to see in a new way and to look at things in a new way under the guidance of God. "I will lead the blind by a road they do not know; by paths they have not known I will guide them. I will turn the darkness before them into light, the rough places into level ground. These are the things I will do, and I will not forsake them" (Is 42:16).

So often we think we see, appreciate, and know God; we accumulate information from reading, studying, discussing, and sharing. But we can never know God unless God enlightens us and grants us knowledge of divine life. This takes place in the dark times of our spiritual journey. These dark nights take place in a later stage of prayer when God teaches us the essence of faith and we entrust ourselves to God's love. "If I say, 'Surely the darkness shall cover me, and the light around me become night,' even the darkness is not dark to you; the night is as bright as the day, for darkness is as light to you" (Ps 139:11-12). However, the joy of coming into the light is never as great as when we have been in darkness. In darkness we find how small our image of God is, and we discover the absolute conviction of divine transcendence and we experience our faith.

It is mysterious how we gain illumination in darkness. After the basic experiences of prayer and meditation, when we are actively involved, God takes over in a new kind of prayer that is a passive experience. We call this prayer contemplation and it happens to us in two phases. The first, a phase of infused recollection and beginning contemplation—namely that experienced by beginners as they move to being proficient in the spiritual life—this happens to many people. The second phase—that which purifies the spirit and prepares it for union with God through love occurs for only a few on their journey from proficients to the deeper union. While contemplation is a gift, we can prepare for it. Centering prayer is a method that helps one prepare for contemplation, whereas contemplation is passively received, a gift of God's Holy Spirit. It is very important to us for contemplation facilitates the purification of faith, hope, and love in preparation for union with God. Contemplation is God's invitation to welcome the divine love in our hearts. To do this we must let God first empty us so that we can be filled.

In the darkness, we can easily feel helpless, abandoned, and no longer standing on firm ground, until we realize it is the brightness of God's revelation that blinds us. In the darkness of contemplation, which is an intimate experience, we gain knowledge of God, and this knowledge is the goal of all faith. These experiences give us profound reasons for faith.

Journeying through the nights is a painful and bewildering experience. People experience it in varied ways, although it will eventually affect every aspect of one's personality—psychological, spiritual, mental, emotional, and even physical. While it is not the same for any two people, it does manifest itself in some common experiences of darkness, pain, emptiness, abandonment, poverty, and nakedness. It is a dispossession of everything we held dear and a reshaping and redirection of the principal energies of the soul. We always think we know what faith is, but we never do unless God teaches us. We never get to know God; it is always God who gets to know us and reveals divine life to us (Gal 4:9).

However, nowadays the metaphor of the night has expanded beyond a personal experience to include social, ecclesial, and political elements that affect us every day. So, we now speak about dark nights in society and in the Church. At times, we experience a loss of previous values that we held dear in society and in the Church and then also experience a great void, emptiness, and lack of conviction that what we thought was so valuable no longer is. We experience a darkness that we cannot remove, but know that only God can do this for us. Sometimes we protect ourselves by believing in an unreal God, one who is remote, angry, a lawgiver, and a judge. Other times we escape into entertainment, endless shopping, drugs, alcohol, gambling, social media, and so on. Only by enduring the darkness of faith can we come to believe in a God of total love, and we must respond with strong love. Then, faith challenges us to think and want only what God thinks and wants.

New ways of experiencing faith

"As you therefore have received Christ Jesus, continue to live your lives in him, rooted and built up in him and established in the faith as you were taught" (Col 2:6-7)

We must always be aware of the limitations of our ways of speaking about God or describing experiences of God. All these can get in the way of encountering God as God is. God is total mystery, unfathomable and unknowable. We must never substitute any idea or understanding for God, no matter how wonderful we think our interpretation might be. Let us always remember that no creature, no human feeling or experience, no idea or dogma, no vision or spiritual ecstasy, no matter how profound, can ever represent or communicate the full reality of God as God is. Therefore we can never afford to become fixated on such things to the point where we confuse them with the true object of our faith.

Our spiritual journey to God is sometimes described as a journey of faith, or a journey of love, or the seeking of God through the nights to union. It is also possible to see the whole spiritual journey as the purification, redirection, and transformation of the spiritual faculties of intellect, memory, and will. People who dedicate themselves to God generally think they know God, possess God, and love God, but this knowledge, possession, and love is so far from authentic that it is damaging to one's faith and pursuit of God. They might even end in believing in a God of their own creation. The intellect can accumulate knowledge, the memory can gather all its wonderful images, and the will can focus on its many loves, but together these do not correspond to God. The work of purifying these faculties begins in contemplation when God teaches us how to know, possess, and love God. We cannot be in union with God in this life through understanding, or through enjoyment, or through imagination, or through any other sense; but only in faith, hope and love. The intellect, memory, and will must turn away from their normal objects of knowledge, possessions, and loves to focus instead on faith, hope, and charity. We know more about God in faith than in the accumulation of knowledge. We possess God more in hope than we do in memories. We love God more in charity than we do in accumulated desires and small loves. So, in faith we find a new way of knowing God, in hope a new way of possessing God, and in charity and new way of loving God.

At first the three theological virtues cause emptiness, confusion, and darkness in the intellect, memory, and will, leading a person to abandon all previous knowledge, possessions, and loves. The spiritual journey implies emptying ourselves of all that is not God, so we can attain what is truly of God. The three spiritual faculties suffer when they are empty, but they must be emptied of false values in order to be filled with new ways of knowing, possessing, and loving God. When they are empty and purified they feel intense pain at their own emptiness and yearn for what they lack, namely God. The intellect thirsts for divine wisdom. The will hungers for the perfection of love. The memory seeks the possession of God in hope.

In the dark experiences of our spiritual journey when God takes over our personal guidance, the spiritual faculties are emptied of false knowledge in the intellect, false hopes in the memory, and false loves and desires in the will. They experience profound pain in their emptiness and can easily be tempted to fill the void with all kinds of false gods. They are in pain because they long for God to fill them with authentic knowledge, hope, and love. With the union with God, the pain of emptiness and longing at times gives way to satisfaction, fullness, and delight, as God transforms the spiritual faculties, filling them with divine communications through the revelation of divine life. Now the pain of emptiness gives way to the joy of fulfillment, and one's intellect, memory, and will are now God's.

So, a person experiences God in the very depths of the soul, where he or she feels transformed and gifted with new knowledge in faith, possession in hope, and love in charity. The spiritual faculties are now illuminated from the inside, rather than as formerly from the outside. Now a person can give to God a genuine appreciation of who God is, returning to God what he or she has received. So, now the intellect receives divine wisdom, being made one with God's intellect, the will is united to goodness and loves as God loves, and the memory is transformed in hope. The person now knows, loves, and hopes, having experienced vitally the divine attributes. In his or her deepest regions of inner spirit a person is transformed in God. The whole journey of the spiritual life consists in this transformation of the spiritual faculties. In this transformation a person learns new ways of knowing, hoping, and loving God. This is a passive experience in which God is the teacher and guide. It is the time when a person becomes his or her true self by identifying totally with God's revelation. This is the goal of faith.

Growth of faith in darkness is a journey of love

"Let love be genuine; . . .Never flag in zeal, be aglow with the Spirit, serve the Lord" (Rom 12:9-12)

We must ask ourselves whether emphasizing the journey of faith is enough, and we find it is not. The original faith-filled experience is an awareness of God's love for us all and of each of us in particular. The journey of love includes an anxious search for God and divine love and includes a lot of pain in unfulfilled longings and the dissatisfaction we feel. This is sometimes followed by the joy of encounter with God but also includes accompanying preoccupation at the possibility of future loss of this satisfying encounter. In spiritual life human beings long for total union with God and the joy and benefits of this love, both in this life and more so in the next. If the journey of faith is the purification of our knowledge of God and of our ways of knowing God, then the journey of love is the purification of our love of God and of our ways of loving God.

During this journey of love we generally have three different experiences, all contributions to our ways of loving God, and all deepen faith. First, there is the love experienced in absence: when God seems absent from us, we can experience God's transcendence and this challenges faith. Second, there is the love experienced in union: in union we feel God present in everything and find that true love is participation. This is a time to experience God's love and goodness. Third, there is the experience of absence even when we are in union. In loving union we realize our own insufficiencies and unworthiness, anxiety rises, and we feel absence at a deeper level even though we are in union, for the union is not permanent.

When all is said and done, our faith is in the overwhelming gift of God's love for us. This is never a merely believed-in love but the pursuit of union. In our spiritual journey through life the greatest motivator to faith is the shocking awareness that God loves us, and we experience this unconditional love in a variety of ways as we have seen in earlier chapters. We are not called to be simply people of faith but people who experience the transforming power of love which is the basis of our faith. We must become the people we are called to be and testify to it. We must overcome childish approaches to religion and mature as human beings aware of our destiny in a vision of love—this is the most important doctrine of faith. Religion's trivia need to be discarded as we center our lives on allowing God to transform us in faith, hope, and charity. This awareness disrupts our ways of thinking, challenges our views of religion, and clarifies how we understand our own destiny. With the psalmist we pray, "May God send his truth and his love," and then with him insist, "My heart is ready, O God, my heart is ready" (Ps 57:3. 7).

As we seek reasons to believe we find that our journey through the dark nights of faith immerses us in levels of awareness and understanding we never anticipated. We may have thought we were working hard in our spiritual lives, struggling to know and love God. Then, we find it is God who is the first lover, seeking us out, filling us with blessings and assuring us of divine love. We become so aware of God's love all around us that it becomes impossible not to believe. After all, the journey of love does not deal with our increasing love for God but it deals with us becoming increasingly aware of God's love for us.

In contemplative prayer with its darkness and enlightenment God teaches us to leave aside all old ways of knowing, possessing, and loving God and we discover we are immersed in God. We find new ways of encountering God, and find we know God in the ways God treats us. We know God is just, merciful, forgiving, enriching, and so on, because God shows all these qualities to us. We do not simply intellectually know God embodies these qualities; rather we experience them in the way God deals with us.

Our journey of faith and love is filled with reasons to deepen our commitment to a life based on a vision and experience of a deep relationship between God and us. Our own spiritual journey gives us so many reasons to deepen faith as we understand and experience that God is vitally interested in each of us. We are not alone and sometimes we feel it, we know it.

As we journey to God we enter times of darkness, emptiness, and sometimes pain. We find God is different than we thought! We can feel lost and discouraged and even doubt our faith in God. But darkness is good for us; it helps us get rid of false images and understandings of God, and it helps us gain illumination regarding who God is and wants to be for us in our faith. It is in darkness that we discover God and find authentic faith.

Personal reflection

Since the 1970s I have come to treasure darkness and its centrality to faith. It is beneficial for all of us to leave the artificial lights of belief systems that are meant to encourage false confidence and pseudo religion. A poet said, "Night is God's most beautiful creation." How true that is! However, I find I must let the darkness of night purify and redirect to a new source of light. I hope I will never be afraid of the dark nights of faith. They are the best sources of new light and illumination I will ever discover.

Questions for discussion or personal reflection

1. Do you think you have made progress in your spiritual life? If yes then how, if no then why?

2. Describe the struggles you experience in trying to be a better Christian.

3. Have you learned new ways of knowing, possessing, and loving God –different than say ten years ago?

Chapter Ten

EXPERIENCING THE TRANSFORMING POWER OF LOVE

Faith in a loving God

"Let thy steadfast love, O Lord, be upon us, even as we hope in thee" (Ps 33:22)

When we think about the many reasons for believing, one set that stands out is our experience of God's love in our daily lives. The love of God that we see and experience urges us to proclaim our faith. After all, faith centers on our experience of God, on our knowledge, possession, and love of God through faith, hope, and charity. We know God in God's love for us, and this spurs us to faith. It seems strange to speak of God who loves, forgives, shows compassion, challenges growth, and shows interest in our daily lives. But, this is God's strategy of love towards us all and in doing this God becomes our model of life.

How can God be the model for our own journey through life? What is the relationship between faith in God and the way we live? What can we discover about ourselves from looking at the life of God, of the three persons of God? Some religions present an understanding of God which is quite apart and disconnected from the rules and regulations they use to direct the faithful in their daily lives. They do not base or model morality and discipleship on their image or understanding of God. Christianity does, and its revelation begins with an experience of a human being, Jesus of Nazareth, and his teachings and way of life: "Everyone then who hears these words of mine and acts on them will be like a wise man who built his house upon rock" (Mt 7:24). However, Jesus is not content to be a wise man or prophet. He tells us that his life and teaching include revealing the ways of the Father: "All things have been handed over to me by my Father; and no one knows the Son except the Father, and no one knows the Father except the Son and any one to whom the Son chooses to reveal him" (Mt 11:27). In fact, in John's gospel Jesus tells Philip: "whoever has seen me has seen the Father" (Jn 14:9). Moreover, before his departure Jesus promises the presence of the Paraclete to continue his revelationary guidance. Christian followership, then, whether individual or communal, is based on the revealed portraits of Father, Son, and Holy Spirit, and it calls all of us to model our lives on the qualities of God that these portraits demand: "Be perfect, therefore, as your heavenly Father is perfect" (Mt 5:48); "Learn from me, for I am gentle and humble in heart" (Mt 11:29); "If we live by the Spirit, let us also be guided by the Spirit" (Gal 5:25). Faith in God leads us to share in God's life of love. We find that faith is not based on a set of teachings but on the call to deepen a relationship with God in Christ.

So the image of God on which we Christians base our lives is Trinitarian—three Persons in one God, whose relationships with one another constitute their very being for all eternity. Therefore, any one-sided representations of God or watered-down understandings of the Trinity produce inauthentic understandings, false societal structures, and unbalanced approaches to spirituality. An authentic theology of Trinity is not abstract but impacts every aspect of our lives. Yet the role of love in the Trinity throws light on our search for deeper understanding in our own spiritual journey. The Trinity implies being constantly present to one another, the intimacy of immediacy, absolute reciprocity, and the centrality of community life. This emphasis on union and relatedness makes love the single great quality that unites us, as it does the Trinity. We are to be present to others and to the world in a transforming way that shows how love constitutes our very being. This is our faith.

The Trinity constantly gives and receives fullness of life through eternity. Constantly drawing others into this fullness, God is lovingly involved in the growth of each and every one of us. That is why we Christians build our lives on genuine hope and see all growth in love as growth in the Lord. So the Trinity is also the model and benchmark for our spiritual commitment. A first century writer, Diadochus of Photice, concluded, "The measure of people's love for God depends upon how deeply aware they are of God's love for them."

God is love and is the model for our spiritual journey through life. We have faith in a loving God. If we truly love God and strive never to fail in the pursuit of love, we can make this journey with confidence for it is not an arduous undertaking in which we scramble to take a few steps forward. Rather, we are being drawn by the love of God who is always the primary Lover. We cannot achieve this ourselves, but we can prevent it from happening. This will be a painful journey for God does not love like we do, and our journey is learning how to love as God wills. Our commitment begins with the realization of our call, and we must deliberately reflect on this awesome reality. We believe we have a personal calling to union with God in love, and to model our lives on God's ways of loving. If we have not thought of this before, then it implies a new perception of our life, identity, and destiny.

This sense of identity and enduring purpose comes from the inward journey into our hearts to discover our hopes, dreams, and deepest longings. Ultimately, spiritual growth is what God is doing in us, and so we will need to appreciate the sense of mystery of our life and surrender to this calling to pursue a life totally given to love. God seeks to create us in God's own image and likeness. We must match God's gift of selfless love with our own choice to focus exclusively on a life of love, for to strive for union in love is our enduring purpose in life, and this is what must motivate us in all we do. This transformation is God's work and we surrender to the divine action within us. So, our faith is rooted in a loving God and we model our daily lives on God's life and ways of loving.

Loving with a heart that is free

"You will need endurance to do God's will and gain what he has promised" (Heb 10:36)

The development of love is only possible in a heart that is free and has overcome or controlled all attachments to false and small loves. Love can easily be distributed and dispersed among many secondary loves that drain the unique total and exclusive love that is needed in the spiritual journey. Jesus insisted on this total commitment when he taught us, "You shall love the Lord your God with all your heart, and with all your soul, and with all your strength, and with all your mind" (Lk 10:27). So, in the pursuit of love that is unified and total we must train ourselves to abandon secondary loves as ends in themselves in order to prove our total dedication to the love of our lives. This implies renunciation, but the ability to renounce something is a characteristic of authentic love. The pursuit of a single-focused love, exclusive, and total is a form of self-surrender that is characterized by fortitude, and perseverance. God's love for us is genuine, tender, supreme, and generous, and we strive to imitate this in our own lives. However, this total surrender is not earned by us but caused by God within our hearts in contemplative prayer. It is a gift of consuming love that includes the desire that every expression becomes an act of love. This is the faith that motivates us in all we do.

So, faith requires a spiritual journey that is a journey of love, and one who makes this journey will need strong love. As we journey, we come to realize that we were created for this love. During the experiences of this journey our love will mature as we learn to let go of false loves and to discover new ways of loving. However, from the first step we must do everything under the powerful motivation of strong love. We need readiness to persevere in this love, and we must sacrifice and do everything to gain or receive it. To the initial determined self-gift and self-forgetfulness needed to start this journey, we will have to add acceptance of the burning pain that love causes. Intense love such as this requires freedom and fortitude as we seek to surrender ourselves to God, to love God in every way we can, and to continue to prepare ourselves to love more purely and intensely. This includes having no loves instead of God. What and who we love form part of an integrated and total dedication to God. We do not abandon other loves but integrate them into one God-directed life. What we cannot do is let any love become an end in itself moving us away from God, substituting for God, and being in competition with God.

Before we feel love in our hearts there is the pain and darkness of the absence of love and a void in our whole purpose in life. We experience a longing at the unfulfilled love that forces us to ask why we feel this way. There is a pain at the need and loss. Small loves, no matter how many, do not satisfy and they pass. The sense of absence remains and will remain until we discover the satisfaction of the love that God offers. When we become aware of these developments in our spiritual lives we find further reasons for faith. It is important to appreciate the difference between choice-directed love and accumulated love. Every day, it is possible to accumulate small signs of love for someone, or in a religious context for God. This process is good but it never impacts one's personality. Making small gestures of love does not cost very much. The search, encounter, union, and mutual possession of authentic love are achieved through choice-oriented decisions that imply painful renunciations that shape the personality of one who seeks God. We mature in spiritual life by making choices that are guided by a single-minded and single-hearted love. This is a fundamental choice always to make decisions in light of the love of our lives. It is insufficient to claim we believe in the importance of love. We must make decisions that prove it and achieve it. Of course, we are not earning this growth in love but are allowing God to make these decisions in and through us and thus removing all obstacles to this divine action within us.

We pray for God's help in the pursuit of love, knowing God will always be with us when we seek deeper love—even though we might not feel it at the time. We can do everything for the love of God, and dedicate ourselves totally to the discovery of the God of love. Sometimes we think our sins hold us back, or that God is reluctant to grant us this gift of love. We might even think God is waiting for our good works or desires to see greater commitment to the sufferings that lead to love. Then again we remember that there is no reason for God to wait, we are not earning anything; everything is gift anyway. We cannot free ourselves from lowly ways of loving unless God achieves this for us. We must never accept anything less than this total gift of God's love and be always ready to receive it. This is the life of faith to which we are called.

Choosing love above all else

"How precious is thy steadfast love, O Lord" (Ps 36:7)

Life is so empty for so many! We give meaning to our lives by daily rebuilding and strengthening faith through daily choices for love; we love day by day and step by step. We need to reaffirm our faith in love even when we see it is absent all around us and denied to those who need it most; denied by those who need it desperately. If we become hardhearted because of self-love we start a process of self-degradation and become ever more coldhearted and cannot get out of it without God's help. However, the evil intolerance and lack of respect for humanity that we see all around us should be addressed by us, individually and as community. If we are aflame with love we become soft and gentle, meek, humble, and patient. In the evening of life we will be judged on our love (John of the Cross), and so we should learn to love as God desires, for one who loves never grows tired in his or her dedication. Love leads to detachment and imitation of the Lord's suffering and self-sacrifice, and then such love protects us from sin. The love of God in one who is faith-filled is almost a continual response. When we reach and practice the love of God, it helps us control the movements of sin and it overflows in love of neighbor.

The entire spiritual journey as a manifestation of faith consists in preparation and purification in view of a union of love. It is above all a transformation that takes place in contemplation when we become receptive to God's activity within us, when God purifies our false desires, false loves, and false gods and fills us with an inflow of love. Our capacity for this love depends on the exclusive and integrated focus of every aspect of our lives. This is a time of mutual surrender, profound communication, and total dedicated devotion to God's service. This is what we can call strong love. A major change takes place in this communion of love; from now on the person's love will be God loving in the person—and this is the work of the Holy Spirit. As a person is thus transformed, all his or her actions cease to be his or her own, for it is the Holy Spirit who now makes them and moves the person to union with God. In one who is filled with faith, God communicates a new way of living and loving, and establishes an intimate relationship with each of us. It is this stronger love and more unitive love that leads the person to God. When God loves others in us and through us, we see the transformative and redemptive power of love.

Spiritual life is a long journey in which this love matures gradually. One's capacity for love depends on the exclusive and integrated focus of every aspect of one's love. This call to love God is the call we never thought we would ever get. This love gives meaning to life. We can try anything and everything else, but we will always come back to this conviction that love alone gives meaning to life.

As we journey, we find the generosity and goodness of many people impress us very positively. In fact, we quickly realize that the people we admire most are those who are known for their love, not their wealth or their skill or their power. It is not that we do not appreciate greatness, creativity, and artistic brilliance, but love is different. Why is it that we humans appreciate love so much when we give or receive it? Is it because love is a manifestation of what is deepest within us, most like what we know we need to be?

Our uncommon journey as Christians to our fulfillment as human beings is a journey to a deeper understanding of the centrality of love in our lives. Christian spirituality, then, is our search for this love and our way of striving for a greater share in God's existence. Our spirituality is rooted in a faith experience but brings that faith to birth in the ever-changing circumstances of modern life. Our pursuit of this goal of making love the central feature of our spirituality must permeate every aspect of life. Christian spirituality today stresses the inner journey to self-discovery. Deep within each one of us there is a zone that is naturally divine, where we encounter ourselves searching for love and in the process encounter the God of Love searching for us. Thus, spirituality gives meaning to our very existence.

Transforming life with love

"Everyone will know that you are my disciples, if you have love for one another" (Jn 13:35)

Faith is based on our experience of God's love. We cannot merely believe in the power of love, we must act on that conviction and show our dedication in action. This means making decisions based on the most loving thing to do. When we live in this way, we ourselves are the first focus of transformation. We change our own attitudes to life, rejecting selfishness, greed, and self-satisfaction, and thus we move away from self-centeredness to self-transcendence. This is a rigorous self-training and eventually leads to the integration of all aspects of life in loving self-gift to God. This single-hearted pursuit of the way of love transforms our decisions, actions, and what we see as our purpose in life.

When we are motivated by our conviction of the transforming value of love, we treat others with a natural benevolence. We wish them well before any encounter, appreciate the good in others, and presume that they will do good. This positive, optimistic approach to others, this "bearing with one another in love" (Eph 4:2), has a healing effect on relationships and opens up the development of friendships that are mutually enriching. The development of love-based friendships prepares us for our journey of love and the fostering of deeper relationships with other people in community and with God.

This new approach to God is based on Jesus' own relationship to his Father. "As the Father has loved me, so I have loved you; abide in my love" (Jn 15:9). It becomes an ever deepening relationship between us as disciples and Jesus. "Abide in me as I abide in you" (Jn 15:4). Believing in the power of love, we become ever more aware that we must make every effort possible to maintain this relationship, knowing that like branches we draw life from union with the vine.

Abiding in God's love is not passive but implies a dynamic ongoing fidelity to the vision of faith. It is an awareness of the presence and power of the Spirit of God within us. It means being faithful to Jesus' teachings, especially the greatest commandment to love one another. Our daily dedication to faithfully live Jesus' teachings and to love one another shows we cherish our faith and we believe in the power of love. At a time when there is so much hatred in our world, we Christians can take a prophetical stance and proclaim by words and deeds the value of living together in faith-filled love.

We discover there is a mutual interrelationship between learning from our experience of God's love for us and how that impacts our relating to God. Our affectivity should not be divided between several objects but integrated into one total self-commitment in love that changes every aspect of our relating both to this world and to a world beyond this one. So we can learn from our experience of God's love how we ought to love others unconditionally, respecting them, forgiving their failures, finding their best gifts, sharing with them as God has done for us. Then we can learn in interaction with others what they hope for, how they seek meaning in life, why they value mutuality, and then we can bring all these learning moments into our own relating to God.

Abiding in Jesus' love means dedicating ourselves to the service of others in society. Jesus came to bring us the Father's love and insisted he came to serve others and thus give an example of the implications of love. He washed the disciples' feet during the Last Supper as a symbolic action of the consequences of love. So, abiding in love leads to a leavening effect on the whole of society and thus manifests the power of love. When in faith we experience the transforming power of love we feel impelled to extend that faith in love to others.

Generally, a faith-filled experience is an experience of abiding in God's love. It may last only a short time, but it produces an understanding of the real values of life. It is an intimacy which changes all future relating to God and to others because of our new relationship with God. When we experience the love of God it strengthens our faith. It is not just a believed-in love but a genuine experience of the living God. Let us remind ourselves constantly that the experience of the transforming power of love is the basis for all faith.

Personal reflection

As I review the happenings in our world, immersed as it is in polarization, violence, and programmed hatred, Christianity has a message that is clearly the answer to this world's needs; a message that is redemptive. I find more and more that faith in a loving God and lives based on that faith and conviction can alone transform our world. Jesus was clear that others will come to believe because of the quality of Christians love. I wish we would give it a chance.

Questions for discussion or personal reflection

1. How strong is your personal relationship with Jesus?

2. Are you and your friends genuine models of Christian love?

3. Describe someone you know who seems to have little or no love in life and try to explain what it is so.

Part III
FINDING LIFE AND FULFILLMENT IN GOD

AN AGENDA FOR THE COURAGEOUS

Living motivated by faith is increasingly difficult in our contemporary Church and world. We are surrounded by dysfunctional organizations, selfishness, hatred, and bigotry. We have seen a few of the many aspects of contemporary religion that undermine good people's desires and efforts to respond to the call of faith. Fortunately, there are many glimpses of grace around us that call us to faith and nurture the faith we struggle to maintain. In this third section we look to several aspects of our faith that help us find life and fulfillment in God. Being faithful to a God-centered life itself nurtures that life. Perhaps we do not give the life that results from faith sufficient opportunity to grow. Maybe our own half-heartedness blocks the growth of faith. In this section we look at a few of the components of our faith and reflect that an enthusiastic commitment to what we claim to believe draws us into a life of faith and strengthens it.

Faith demands a conversion and change of life that lead to a spiritual growth that makes faith real. When we journey to God along these paths God reveals aspects of the life of faith to us that enthuse us and encourage us to strive for deeper knowledge and experience of God. We do this in a particular way in prayer. Often our prayer is a shadow of what it should be. When we give ourselves to growth in prayer and to allowing God to facilitate that growth, we find God fulfills our hopes and reveals the divine life to us. The organizational part of contemporary Church life is filled with problems, some of which block faith, but the core values of community life as Jesus intended it can nourish faith and help maintain its relevance. God blesses each of us with many powers that manifest faith and enrich it too. These energies of the soul are often left untapped, but when we use them with dedication they make us the people of faith we want to be. Above all, faith is centered on Jesus Christ, the revealer and sustainer of our spiritual lives. If we let him become the center of all we do our faith grows and finds deeper meaning. In this third part let us look at these various aspects of the life of faith and re-commit ourselves to living them with greater dedication.

In part I we tried to honestly consider the struggles we face in our modern world and Church. In part II we found we needed more time and reflection in our reading to identify convincing reasons for faith and to make them our own. Here, as we read part III, we will need deep and prolonged meditation on these chapters to immerse ourselves with enthusiasm in a re-dedication to faith. Perhaps readers might be willing to read small sections at a time to think seriously about the level of their dedication to these various aspects of the life of faith.

Chapter Eleven

DEDICATING OURSELVES TO SPIRITUAL GROWTH

Conversion to the values of faith

"The time is fulfilled, and the kingdom of God is at hand;
repent, and believe in the gospel" (Mk 1;15)

Amidst the many problems we face in struggling with faith, along with the many reasons we can find to believe, there are several experiences that give us life and fulfillment in God. Among the many gifts God grants to each of us is the call to conversion. We sense this call in the depths of our hearts and know it comes from beyond us and is real. Conversion means a change of heart, as long as we remember that in Jesus' time heart was considered to be the source of both emotions and knowledge—and so conversion came to mean accepting a totally new outlook on life. The new outlook on life centers on faith in

Jesus. Disciples who have a special relationship with him establish a fellowship among themselves in a community of followers of shared faith. Jesus always takes the initiative in calling people to faith, to discipleship, and to the centering of life on him. He becomes our teacher, guide, support, and challenge. For our part as disciples, we must repent of former failed choices, change the direction of our lives, dedicate ourselves in obedience to Jesus, build on his words, and accept the sacrifices of life in his name. These are the living consequences of faith. We know that as disciples our response to the Lord's call leads to the rejection of evil, painful choices, confession of the Lord, and a commitment to holiness of life. It also means joining the community of believers, publicly witnessing to the priorities of the Lord, and becoming salt of the earth and light for the world (Mt 5:13-14).

Our commitment to Jesus has two phases—turning away from sin and evil and turning towards God. The former is often referred to as repentance and the latter conversion. True conversion is indistinguishable from discipleship. Those who accept this change of direction or change of outlook in life enter into union with Jesus that anticipates the future kingdom—an age of light, life, love, and truth. As disciples, we are drawn by the initiative and love of the Father, and we deliberately make the choice to live under the guidance of the Spirit and in light of the world to come. This changes everything for the disciple whose life is now totally directed to God (Jn 6:68-69). This is what faith is all about. In pursuing this conversion we find life and fulfillment in God.

Conversion is a spiritual awakening—an interior renewal—that challenges us to reject our false selves and false values and instead live by the values of the Spirit. So, it calls us as disciples to live on a new plane of being and actions, allowing ourselves to be influenced by God and by values of a horizon of life beyond this one. In other words, we are influenced by our experience of faith. It is an opportunity to get to know God, while at the same time getting to know others and ourselves—maybe for the first time. This means that as disciples we strive to live in opposition to sin in its many forms, both personal and communal. It also means acquiring knowledge of God in Jesus Christ—again maybe for the first time. In conversion we find a new way of believing, living, and discovering that Jesus is the way, the truth, and the life. "Very truly, I tell you, anyone who hears my word and believes him who sent me has eternal life, and does not come under judgment, but has passed from death to life" (Jn 5:24).

Jesus considered that everyone needed to be called to repentance otherwise their hearts naturally focused on lesser values. This death to false values and resurrection to new life with God is particularly important today when men and women frequently seem to embrace wrong emphases in their lives and justify them as faith. Everywhere there are signs of this drift away from authentic values of the Spirit and towards a situation of disorder. In earlier chapters of part one we saw failures in religion; corruption, sexual perversion, hypocrisy, lives of luxury, self-righteousness, and so on. To these we can add examples from contemporary society; moral depravity, oppression of the poor, denial of human rights, lack of truth, genocide, leadership without service, need to control, greed, militarism, and so on. Our lives ought to be God-centered but when left to ourselves we seem more frequently to focus on self-centered false values and the comfort of religion.

So, many people today give the impression they believe that a person gets better by accumulating good things and practices—prayers, devotions, retreats, projects, ministry, movements, and so on. However, a person is not the sum of components—he or she does not get better by adding on or accumulating more religion and its devotions. A person finds his or her authentic self by removing all the false approaches to life and finding God in the depths of his or her heart. "Create in me a clean heart, O God, and put a new and right spirit within me" (Ps 51:10). This is precisely what happens in conversion—the turning away from mundane values and the discovery that the new life God gives us is to be found deep within our own hearts. Peter, in his first letter, refers to the former as the useless way of life and the latter as a life when we become obedient to the truth. Paul, writing to the Romans, refers to the former as our imprisonment and the latter as the new spiritual way. In the simplest contemporary terms, conversion is a movement away from self-centered living and a move to self-transcendence. Experiencing God active within us is a confirmation of our faith. We need to stress that in conversion we are looking for the vision of God, no one else's. This means we have to find out what God wants of us and this will include reading, reflection, study, sharing, and prayer. Only genuine discernment can lead us to an appreciation of the vision of God to which we are called— that is the new outlook on life that we seek as a result of conversion.

Christian Spirituality

"I have come that you may have life and have it to the full"
(Jn 10:10)

Spirituality is the life that results from conversion and faith. After a faith-filled experience we sense we must live differently. Spirituality deals specifically with the stages of growth in a God-directed life and the maturing of values proposed by God in Christ and appreciated in faith. As we try to live out the heart of our faith we find in spiritual life there are some values that are perennial— the Beatitudes, need of prayer, self-sacrifice, and the challenges of the Sermon on the Mount, and so on. There are others that change as our situations and circumstances change—how to live these values in modern society with changes in relationships, with our technological society, with growth in political rights, with new forms of business and economic development. Moreover, there are ways and methods that also vary to preserve the unchanging values and to live them in relevant ways for changing times. Through our spiritual development we make our faith real each day.

Spirituality, as a specific branch of theology, never refers to static concepts but only to dynamic ones. It is not interested in prayer but growth in prayer, not charity but growth in charity, not social justice but growth in our commitment to social justice. Faithful following of a call from God in Christ leads us to find fulfillment, and to a dedication that makes a qualitative difference in the way we behave in our daily lives. This gives us values, vision, purpose, and perspective on life—all the results of faith. It opens the way to the fullest and deepest values of human growth, the profound and intimate values we cherish most: the yearning for self-fulfillment, for community, and for transcendence—values that prove our faith. Rooted in the message of Jesus, Christian spirituality studies the growth of the person from God's perspective. Spirituality is more than a segment of life, a Sunday addition, it is a way of viewing the whole of life. We live differently because of our faith. Spirituality can offer us a strategy for growth in faith while appreciating that each individual's way to human-Christian maturity may vary. Christian spirituality brings life and growth into authentic focus as it highlights the genuine concerns of life and human hope. It aims to integrate the unique message of Jesus with the best of all human values. This dedication to faith brings the best out of us and can give us an exciting and fulfilling life in response to faith.

Spirituality for us as people of faith is the interaction of God's gift of transforming life with our efforts in concrete circumstances of each day. Thus, it is always a transitory manifestation of perennial values. Rooted in the great tradition of Christ's message, we cannot allow it to degenerate into religious fads while neglecting essential values of faith. Faced with our own emptiness, we need to be open to grace and to develop the faith-filled skill of waiting for God's interventions, together with an attitude of readiness to receive God's gifts and use them creatively. Contemporary spirituality concerns itself with the concrete circumstances of our own age, and stresses spontaneity, personal authenticity, global vision, and vital needs.

Recent spiritual renewal focuses on a rediscovery of the essential source values of faith and an opening to the autonomous values of the world. So, authentic faith is not an escape from this world but a way of living our humanity to the fullest. Spirituality includes an awareness of personal responsibility for others, and a new community consciousness in believers. Contemporary developments in spirituality have led us to new ways of thinking and living Christianity that imply a new value for human and earthly realities—how to live our responsibilities in changing social, environmental, climate, political situations with interconnectedness, awareness of mutualty, technological development, education, and ever increasing social movements for rights, equality, peace, and justice. Spirituality refers to who we are and who we ought to be in Christ. Our spirituality must speak to today rather than to what spirituality was over two thousand years ago. Thus, our faith is a powerful interruption challenging the world's false values and offering a life of prophetical relevance.

Spirituality a journey based on faith

"And this is eternal life, that they know thee, the only true God, and Jesus Christ whom thou hast sent" (Jn 17:3)

Spirituality embraces all of our lives, making sure that every facet responds to the inner call to live our faith fully at any given moment. This implies that our spirituality is all about relationships, with oneself, others, communities, the world around us, and God. It is the ordering of our lives so that the values of the inner self and faith shine forth in all that we do. Jesus Christ said, "I have come that you may have life and have it to the full" (Jn 10:10); and an early Christian writer called Irenaeus said, "The glory of God is when a man or woman is fully alive"; that is the spirituality of real faith! Spirituality is not some non-descript emotional feeling of piety and religious devotion, but it takes as its starting point the concrete circumstances of our daily lives; our lived experience in the world we know. It is a journey in which the best values of humanity, especially faith, hope, and love, help give direction to our lives and help us advance towards achieving the enrichment of an adult personality. It refers to our entire lives based upon decisions that show fidelity to the inner motivation of our lives—that is, our faith. Christian spirituality presumes a positive approach to creation, the world around us, and our human nature created and redeemed by God. Spirituality now refers to making our faith real and effective on a day to day basis. In fact, it is a journey of faith in ourselves, in others, in the goodness of creation, in ultimate values, and in God. Spirituality permeates every moment of every day.

Spirituality is a response to a fundamental demand in the depths of our hearts that urges us to take life seriously, giving primacy to God-directed values. As men and women of faith we reverence these perennial values but interpret them in transitory forms. In fact the exploratory dimension of spirituality preserves its relevance. Christian spirituality must relate these values to present trends and developments. So, we cannot live spiritualities as people in the past lived them. Even our latest understandings and experiences of God can block our encounter with God. Thus, conversion includes a new outlook on religion and its beliefs.

One of the major developments in the last couple of decades has been an extraordinary interest in integrating faith with daily life and activity. Spirituality that results from our faith permeates our commitment to every aspect of life. This results when we realize that all life including our family and working lives with their new focuses of call are always a re-living of the baptismal challenge to belong to Christ, to live and love for him. This leads us to relate differently to self, to others, and even to the cosmos because of a new way of living our relationship to Jesus. The service of others in daily life is a particularly splendid way of realizing this.

The call to live faith will need to be renewed on a daily basis, as we face increasing demands that must never lead to a reduced ideal of our calling. Both feeling called by faith and yearning for personal integration, we as Christians strive to respond each day to the implications of that call we feel deep in our hearts. Spirituality includes a sense of humility, as we struggle daily to become what we hear the Lord calling us to be. For each of us, no period can pass without learning something new either in prayer, in sharing with peers, in ongoing study, in reflective application of the Word of God, and in discussion with other believers. We cannot drift in mediocrity, unfocused and uncaring, without purpose or mission, for this leads to a loss of dedication. Let us reflect on the importance of living our faith in every aspect of our spirituality.

Spirituality is a manifestation of reality and the way in which people can become their true selves in response to God's call. It must be lived by individuals responding to their lives and destiny with God. For each of us God's call in the Lord is to become who we are truly capable of being. Our spirituality must imply constant creativity rather than any acceptance of pre-packaged and recycled spirituality, whether in the form of saints from the past, or spiritual movements of more recent times, or the comforting practices of bourgois religion. We must learn to find and then leave aside the worst of ourselves. Whatever convictions regarding the meaning of life lie at the core of our hearts, conversion implies basing our entire lives on those convictions.

Make faith real

"I am the vine, you are the branches. He who lives in me and I in him will produce abundantly" (Jn 15:5)

The life that results from faith matures in expression as we ourselves mature. This life will be different in early years than in later years; different for less educated than for more educated; different for women than for men, and so on. All of us will seek to manifest in our own originality the faith-experience that transformed our lives. But, new emphases will emerge for all of us. Daily prayers will no longer be as important as fostering a reflective life. Occasional good deeds will no longer be as important as an entire life of goodness for others. Self-denial and self-sacrifice will no longer be as important as being a person for others. Rituals will not be as important as the ecstasy of a profound experience of faith. Accumulating more will be insignificant alongside the building of a life of hope. At the same time, as people committed to spiritual growth we will emphasize simplicity and intensity of the present moment and always remember the faith experience that transformed our lives. We will stress authentic, unconditional love of self, others, the world, and God. Each day we will strive to transcend ourselves and become other-centered and give ourselves to the common good of people everywhere. Then, we will accept the fact that we have a mission and a destiny in this world; personally called by God to help others live life to the full. This call of faith can be truly exciting.

We make our lives of faith real by a conscious personal commitment. Nowadays, faith is a matter of personal choice not an inherited tradition. We are not passive but active in appreciating the importance of responsible dedication. As Christians, this implies a rediscovery of our baptismal vocation, and for others a rediscovery of the initial great call they felt in the moment of faith. Living faith does not refer primarily to the effort we contribute, but rather to what God is doing in us. So, a hallmark of our life of faith is awareness that life is grace and gift of God. Our contribution is to be open, receptive, and aware of our emptiness without God.

Nowadays, our faith calls us to take responsibility for moral choices. As circumstances change our conscience evaluates differently. We facilitate good decisions by self-evaluation, prayer, prudence, knowledge of faith, and consensus of other people of faith. We cannot prove our dedication to a life of faith in our spare time, but only in the major moments of each day. This includes the importance of a right approach to our working life. Our fidelity to the values of spiritual life is severely tested during working hours when we are generally alone. How we deal with work—with honesty, generosity, service, and quality, proves our commitment. The life that results from faith includes a readiness to work for community at all levels—family, friends, Church, political, and international life. Our struggle-filled efforts to build community can bring transformation to every level of life.

An important contemporary aspect of life is joy—enjoying the good things of life. This, too, must become part of a life of faith. We in the developed world are the only generation in human history that has two lives, a working life and a leisure life, and we also need to permeate the latter with the values of faith. We have already considered the importance of reflection and prayer, participation in local religious institutions' life and worship, our outreach in service to others, and a call to challenge the injustices of our world. We will need to develop all these aspects of life that result from faith, so we are always making our faith real.

While being drawn to transcendent life we keep our feet on the ground, and we dedicate ourselves to assuring that our spiritual dedication is made real in the practicalities of daily life. As people of faith we look back to the spiritual experience that transformed our lives and do so with excitement and enthusiasm. We are called to fullness of life, and must never stand still if we wish to get there. We must dedicate ourselves to spiritual growth as a sign of the depth of our faith.

Dedicating ourselves to growth in our spiritual lives is a wonderful way of seeking God. The life that results from faith and its spiritual transformation is our way of becoming who we are capable of being; it is a striving for a greater existence. This life is our way of affirming the values and vision of our faith. Above all, it becomes a way of integrating this present horizon of life with the realm of life beyond this one.

Personal Reflection

I have always found that effort in the spiritual life always has its rewards but never as clearly felt as when I try to be open and receptive. In quiet and receptive times I find a power takes over that is beyond my efforts and gives me insights that I otherwise would never attain. Dedicating ourselves to spiritual growth brings experiences that confirm faith. May we let the Lord lead us to the goals he has for us.

Questions for discussion or personal reflection

1. Do you live differently because you are a person of faith? How?

2. Give examples of conversion in your own life. Ask yourself when you changed direction in your life because of your faith?

3. What does God want of you at this stage in your life?

Chapter Twelve

FOCUSING FAITH IN THE LIFE OF PRAYER

Growth in prayer

"Abide in me, and I in you. . . . As the Father has loved me, so
I have loved you; abide in my love" (Jn 15:4, 9)

As people who have had a faith-filled experience that revealed connections between the here and now and a realm of life beyond the ordinary dimensions of our world, we seek to maintain that link through prayer. Vocal and community prayer can help. But they are too wordy and too full of us to be significant other than as remote forms of prayerful reflection. Prayer is a relationship of love between a person and God. We bridge the span between our life and loving union with God in a life beyond this one through various forms of communication. At first, we tend to fill these times of communication with many words, thoughts, hopes, requests, and promises. However, as time passes, we need to think less and talk less in prayer and just learn how to be quietly present to God. Friends do not need to talk all the time; neither do lovers, nor do people of faith with shared spiritual values. Rather, as time passes, words are less important, and people just like to spend time together with God in prayer.

Being present to God in prayer gradually means letting go of former ways of knowing and loving God and opening our hearts to new experiences. This is a time of simplification of prayer and of the laying aside of prayer structures and methods that we once controlled so well. Prayer gradually consists of few words, few thoughts; it is more a loving attention to God. Put briefly, this stage means talking less to God and loving more.

As we give ourselves to God in prayer, it seems normal to expect that the loving relationship will intensify and unfortunately it generally does not. In the long run it will return in a different form, but not for some time. Dedicated to prayer, we must first enter the darkness that brings disorientation, sadness, pain, insecurity, and even a sense of abandonment. Rather than intensify the relationship of love in prayer, God often withdraws from us, acts differently than we ever expected, seems to withhold love, and leaves us feeling alone. This can cause a sense of crisis in our faith. This is a period of darkness that purifies a human being's way of relating to God. It is a painful experience but one that we will look back on with joy and peace.

In prayer we must be open to receive. Our contribution amounts to removing obstacles of a false self, an inaccurate understanding of prayer, and a too-human perception of God. Our primary response is openness and receptivity, letting God transform us in every aspect of our being. The strategy of giving time to reflection and prayer is a decision for depth, enrichment, and transformation in our spiritual lives. Being constantly connected to God through prayer helps empty us of selfishness and brings us the power to be our true selves.

When we look at prayer in more detail we discover common elements in the spiritual lives of people of faith. God draws us through stages to deeper prayer and union with God.[11] These experiences strengthen our faith. Some of these stages in growth are active—we contribute, and some are passive—God's work within us. Whatever stage we find ourselves in, it is useful and challenging to look ahead to the deeper stages of prayer. Looking at later stages can inspire and challenge us, and make us aware of how God wants to draw us to deeper spiritual life and to reveal clearer knowledge of God's ways.

Active stages in the life of prayer

"Ask, and it will be given to you; seek, and you will find; knock, and it will be opened to you" (Lk 11:9)

The point of departure for all spiritual growth is not us but God. We are not moving forward but being drawn forward. So, we are not moving through various stages in prayer, struggling on our own until we reach the final stage of union. Rather, the point of departure is God who is totally interested in us moving to union in divine life and love. God is the point of departure and comes to our help, drawing us forward through stages of growth, blessing our contributions in the early stages of the spiritual life. These early stages include our efforts, and then God takes over and grants the blessings of the later stages, drawing us to union.

It has always been thought that there are two phases in spiritual life; an active phase and a passive phase. Both are God's blessings to us, but in the first phase our contributions and efforts are important even though our efforts primarily consist in getting out of God's way! We are learning how not be an obstacle to God's work within us. We begin our journey to God by learning three fundamental attitudes that must remain with us throughout our entire lives: love, detachment, and humility. Love is the defining characteristic of a Christian personality, and it can never be absent from anything we do. Detachment simply means we have no interest in anything except a God-directed life. However, every aspect of life must be a part of this, so every aspect of life needs to be integrated into our spiritual development. There is no such thing as religious and non-religious aspects of life; all must be part of our self-gift to God. Humility calls us to keep our feet on the ground ("humus" = earth), get to know ourselves well, be real in everything we do, and be true to ourselves. Authentic religion and spiritual growth is the single best way to be human, to be who we are called to be. These are the three touchstones of spiritual authenticity—love, integration, and realism. Religious and mystical writers can, at times, let themselves be carried away with the language of love and can interpret detachment as self-rejecting approaches to life. These three qualities go together and are mutually sustaining and mutually corrective. Love must be integrative and real. Detachment must be loving and imply a real relationship with this world. Humility must be loving, even of oneself, and imply a real and authentic relationship with every aspect of life. Once these three foundational attitudes are a part of life, we can begin our journey to God, and as we do—with all our efforts—God transforms these efforts with charity, hope, and faith, so that we learn new ways of loving, possessing, and knowing God.

First stage of prayer—vocal prayer.

We express our innermost being through our bodies and our first form of prayerful expression is vocal prayer. This can never be merely mechanical but must always be permeated by thought, reflection, and by always understanding who is speaking to whom—we with all our weaknesses are speaking to God. This stage, along with the next two, is part of a beginner's purification and preparation for future growth. We must purify our negative energies, identify the obstacles we present, and convince ourselves that we have to be different. It is a period when we struggle to reject sin and a world of distractions to pursue the life of grace. We need self-knowledge and humility, and we must be content to be where we are and yet open to be led by God. If we want this vocal prayer and reflection to be part of a serious commitment to spiritual growth we will need a lot of courage, even in this early stage. The problem that can arise is when we who wish to give ourselves to growth in prayer unfortunately develop interests in this world as an end in itself and in its false values that can block our ability to appreciate what lies ahead in the later stages, and we can easily feel helpless and without ability to move ahead. Self-understanding and humility are the dominant needs and achievements of this first stage. Vocal prayer plus reflection is an important first step in prayer. With this prayer we are beginning to think about God and who God is for us; we are reflecting on God's presence to us and our need to think about a realm of life beyond this present one. When we immerse ourselves in this prayer, we should choose a fixed time of adequate length and subject matter that is inspiring. This prayer can easily be a part of a busy life. All we need is a few minutes clearly concentrated on God, or current times of prayer when they are given a new focus.

Second stage of prayer—occasional meditation

As we continue our vocal prayer with reflection, especially when our prayer forms include inspiring and challenging readings and thoughts, it becomes natural enough that we think a little more, try to understand the words we are reciting, savor the sentiments, apply them to ourselves and to our world, and even make resolutions based on them. This step by step process of discursive thought and affective reaction is what we call meditation. At first it happens just now and again, as God uses our efforts to draw us forward. At this point we begin to focus more on truths we encounter in our reflective vocal prayer and especially to center our minds and hearts on the person of Jesus whom we find is accompanying us at every step. In this occasional meditation the Lord is encouraging us to understand spiritual truths and values, to learn more about ourselves and our faults and failings, and to enkindle our energy and affection for an increasingly present, loving God. Even in this early stage of prayer we find something is happening to our minds and our hearts. We also begin to appreciate that our faculties of intellect, memory, and will are focusing differently than previously—more on God and the values of faith than on scattered distractions

Third stage of prayer—habitual meditation and acquired recollection.

When we give ourselves to occasional meditation we more and more try to make a habit of it. Our small efforts and the attraction and blessings of God lead us to make regular meditation an important part of each day. We need to strengthen this commitment with good Christian living, avoidance of even small sin, and a progressive effort to purify failings and re-educate our faculties and senses with self-sacrifice. A key characteristic of this stage is the practice of promptness in obedience to God's will as we begin to obey the demands of grace. Three developments happen to our meditation in stage three: 1. we increase our meditation until it becomes habitual, 2. we decrease the discursive and intellectual aspects of reflection and focus more on the affective dimensions of the concluding part of meditation, and 3. we simplify our meditation in active recollection. So, three components characterize stage three: habitual meditation, affective prayer, and the prayer of simplicity or active recollection.

All meditation should end with acts of love of God—that is the reason for the discursive reflection, to stimulate the will to love. As we become more accustomed to the practice of meditation we decrease the preparatory reflective parts and increase the affective parts, so that the workings of the will take over from the discussions and reflections of the intellect. The more meditation develops, the more love takes over, and gradually we want to conform our will and our way of loving to Christ's.

As meditation becomes habitual and as affective prayer takes over, our meditation also becomes simpler, a form of acquired recollection. In this prayer we recollect our senses, look at the Lord and know he is present to us, and give him our simple, loving attention. Former reasoning and discursive prayer are transformed into a simple loving gaze on God. In this active recollection, which results from our own efforts, we gain a conscious realization of the presence of God. We should cultivate the habit of awareness of the presence of God and maintain companionship with God during the day. We do well to prepare our bodies in stillness, to quiet our minds in peace, to find a sacred space and sacred time, and to recollect, concentrate, and rest in the Lord. Then, we can attentively respond to the Lord, listening, sharing, and expressing our love. If our minds wander, we should try to re-collect ourselves and re-focus on being present to the Lord.

Passive, mystical stages in God's gift of prayer

"For the Father himself loves you, because you have loved me and have come to believe that I came from God" (Jn 16:27)

If we give ourselves to the simple, active stages of prayer, then after a while God takes over—often, but not always. Our prayer then develops an internal dynamic of its own, and we then move forward effortlessly—drawn by God. This can also take place in our normal busy lives. This second phase of prayer is the mystical or contemplative. This is a passive phase and these stages of prayer cannot be acquired. Rather they are completely gift from God. Mysticism refers to the hidden or inaccessible aspects of prayer that we can only encounter due to God's love and blessings. We do not earn contemplation, but God draws us to this new life if God so chooses and if we are prepared and made to have the capacity by God. In contemplation a person experiences that God is present to him or her. It is an immediate and direct contact with God even though it may not be felt or known. It can also be an experience that includes an intuition which is intense, profound, and very simple. In contemplation a person is moved passively by God. This is an experience which is not in words but in love, and so it is ineffable. It is an infusion of knowledge and love and is given in different ways and degrees to people who are particularly purified of self-centeredness, committed to love, and desire only to do the will of God. Contemplation has great sanctifying qualities, as it leads to a renewal of life, to a wisdom in our knowledge of

God, and to union with God in love. It is an enlightenment, an expansion of consciousness, and a great awakening. It produces forgetfulness of self, a desire to do God's will, and a commitment to the service of others. It brings a person inner peace, increased spiritual strength, and personal fulfillment. Contemplative prayer is humanity's greatest opportunity to welcome God into life. This is the light that comes after darkness.

Clearly no one can earn the gift of contemplation, but we can prepare ourselves with the daily dedication to stillness of our bodies, to being open and attentive to the inspirations of the Holy Spirit, to lovingly concentrate on Christ, and to practice silence in God. We can do all this by fostering an awareness of the presence of God, a spirit of recollection, a sense of wonder, a healthy sense of aloneness, and the patience and willingness to wait. All this takes place in the active phase of prayer, what we have seen in the first three stages. However, when all is said and done contemplation is a gift that purifies and transforms our ways of communicating with God, and prepares us for a loving union.

The fourth stage of prayer—the prayer of quiet.

The prayer of quiet is God's work within us. "Quiete" is a Latin word and means "at rest." In this prayer we become "at rest," not actively involved, but passively receiving from God. It is a time when the major spiritual interventions of God begin within us, and we gain a new experience and a new way of knowing God. On our part we need humility, charity, and continued care of the ascetical life. This is a prayer in which the will is passive but not the other faculties of intellect and memory, and it is important that we do not allow ourselves to be distracted by the faculties in such a way that they quench the spark of God's love and gifts. At this time we should not think much but love much. This is a time when virtues grow and understanding deepens—signs of God's special blessings. A problem can arise because of these blessings, namely, many reach this stage, think it is the end, and few pass beyond it. This can also be a time of suffering, sometimes caused because we cannot understand what is happening to us. At this time, perhaps the one thing we can do is to make non-discursive acts of love and commitment.

In the prayer of quiet a person experiences extraordinary peace and pleasure in recognizing God's presence deep within one's inner spirit. It is as if one knows God is present, communicating knowledge and love. In fact, one feels captivated by God's personal presence, deep within one's spirit. At first, this experience may only last a few minutes, but it can also become frequent and eventually habitual. The will is now passive, wanting nothing except to be in this loving and revealing presence. The intellect and memory are still active but more focused on the things of God. The prayer of quiet produces transforming effects in a person—he or she becomes different in spiritual life and commitment because of God's loving and revealing presence. A person who is blessed with the prayer of quiet finds that nothing matters anymore, except to love in this intimate presence with God. This awareness permeates everything a person does. This fourth stage in prayer begins with infused recollection which affects primarily our way of knowing God, moves to the prayer of quiet which affects principally the will, and concludes in the prayer of the sleep of the faculties in which all the faculties are at rest. The next step will be the prayer of union.

Fifth stage of prayer—prayer of simple union.

Spiritual writers distinguish three stages in the prayer of union, three progressive steps towards complete passivity of all spiritual faculties and union with God. They can be understood as three stages in spiritual marriage: courtship, engagement or betrothal, and marriage. The fifth stage in prayer, the prayer of simple union, is a progressive development from the increasing passivity of the faculties when the main faculties of will and intellect are passive. So, at this stage all the spiritual faculties (intellect, memory, and will) are passive, totally centered on union with God—the will loves, the intellect is in awe at the love, and the memory is quietened and non-intrusive, for all are in union with God.

When we say the spiritual faculties are passive we mean the will wants only to love God and not to be distracted by anything else (to be passive to everything except a life of love of God). The memory no longer remembers happy good times of the past but is focused exclusively on possessing God in hope (to be passive to everything else). The intellect only thinks of God and God-directed values and no longer thinks of anything that distracts from God (to be passive to all but God). This does not exclude other aspects of life such as loving relationships, dedicated professionalism, responsible social commitments, and so on. But all these are done according to the will of God and become part of an integral total centering of life on the values of faith.

In this stage a person has no further interest in the things of this world as ends in themselves but abandons itself to God who takes possession of it. This stage of prayer leads to a transformation, but the person in this stage does not really understand what is happening; in fact, a person does not even recognize himself or herself. A person feels he or she is a different person, knowing he or she is now so united to God in love, in obedience to the divine will, and in complete service to others. No matter how wonderful this prayer of union is, it is still just a courtship where two people are getting to know each other and trying to decide if they want to make this relationship permanent. This call to union is the fundamental purpose of life and each of us needs to reflect on our calling and ask for God's grace to be faithful.

Sixth stage of prayer—conforming union.

After the courtship of the prayer of simple union a person makes the final decision to give himself or herself totally to God, pledging commitment and undertaking to direct life according to faith. So, this is a period of intense enjoyment, some anxiety, and final preparations to become transformed and intimately united to each other. In prayer and life, this sixth stage of prayer is a deepening of union of the entire person with God and an intense and painful purification in preparation for final union. The deepening union, sometimes called conforming union, is a development from stage five. In this stage, not only the principal spiritual faculties of intellect, memory, and will but also even external senses are now passive to everything except God—one's entire being is now captivated by God. The key feature of this stage is absorption in God; all faculties and senses are now conformed to God. A person at this time is centered on God and has no interest in anything else, but will readily leave this intense union to go out in service to others when this is one's obligation and God's will. However, this can be painful when one's longing for God is so intense.

This sixth stage leaves a person overwhelmed by joy, peace, and contentment. It produces in the soul great detachment from all that is not God, creates within the soul a yearning for solitude, and encourages an intense desire to love and serve others in God's name. A spiritual person willingly accepts the pain that comes with love. In this union of one's entire being with God the body shares in the delights of the soul. This is a special period of infused contemplation—a time of purification that comes with the pain of longing, and growth in virtue and in love.

Seventh stage of prayer—transforming union.

Many writers refer to this last stage as spiritual marriage because of their conviction that it is a permanent, indissoluble, state of love, and because the seeker and God are made one in mutual surrender. This experience is also called transforming union because the person seeking God is now totally transformed in God. The ecstatic experiences of previous stages are no longer present, trials may still occur, but above all this is a time of permanent peace, a time to experience the full power of God's love, and a time of total immersion and experience of the life and indwelling of the Trinity. Theologians consider that this is a time of confirmation in grace, which does not exclude smaller failings and sins which are part of a just person's daily life. This experience of transforming union in spiritual marriage leads to complete self-forgetfulness for the seeker or lover, a readiness to suffer the pains of love, peace in persecution and trials, a great desire to serve others, and a total integration of everything one does in loving gift to God.

In moving through the stages of growth in prayer we gain more and more knowledge of God who reveals the divine life to us, clarifies the meaning of our faith, and transforms our inner life and daily living, making us the best people we are capable of being. This prayer is not something we earn, rather it happens to us. When we experience this work of God within us, it becomes a powerful confirmation of the reality of faith.

In prayer our faith becomes reality. We encounter God in whom we believe. When we are surrounded by attacks on faith, even from religion, as we saw in earlier chapters, prayer gives us opportunity to meet God who strengthens our faith. In prayer we become alive with awareness, vital knowledge, and transforming experiences of the God of our faith.

Personal Reflection

I know that prayer is not what I am doing but what God is doing in me. I challenge myself to become ever more aware of my calling to prayer. After all, prayer must be able to overwhelm all of us with the happiness of faith and faith-filled love. Like many people, I live with only a shadow of what prayer should be. Let us hope we can all maintain spiritual dedication to the life of prayer amidst the challenges of our very busy lives.

Questions for discussion or personal reflection

1. What is your prayer like? Has it changed and matured as you have grown older?

2. How should we as Church introduce younger people to the life of prayer?

3. What is the purpose of prayer? Do you give it an important role in your life?

Chapter Thirteen
PARTICIPATING IN THE LIFE OF THE CHURCH

From faith in Jesus to life in the Church

"They devoted themselves to the apostles' teaching and fellowship, to the breaking of bread and the prayers" (Acts 2:42)

In the earlier chapters we considered several problems with the organizational Church that can weaken faith. But the Church is entrance to the Kingdom, a community expression of faith, a support and standard of faith. When we stress the best aspects of the Church we can benefit from its many enriching contributions to faith.

In the New Testament we find that the disciples soon became aware that they formed a special group around Jesus, faithful to his teachings and to each other. As Jesus' companions, they were always with him to receive his special teachings. Following Jesus' departure they were convinced that he would return immediately in his Second Coming. When this was delayed each gospel community struggled to provide an answer to what believers should do and how they should live in the time of waiting. This was one of the two great crises in the early Church; why must the Church exist at all? What was unique about the Church's origins and what were the characteristics of its life that needed to be repeated in each successive generation, if believers were to faithfully express what was essential to this communal manifestation of faith? Certainly, the disciples were all aware that the early Church's preaching implied a call to membership in a community, and salvation meant belonging to this community of the saved.

From his first sermons Jesus announced *the coming of the Kingdom of God*, and spoke frequently about it, right up to the eve before his passion, insisting that it was still not here, but after the passion he spoke as if the kingdom were now present. The evangelists suggest that the Kingdom can be seen more globally as the sovereign reign of God, realized fully at the end of time, but anticipated in Jesus. The Church was seen as the door to the Kingdom, but to enter the Kingdom required reform of life, faith in the gospel, and appropriate attitudes and responses in disciples. The early Church thought that the opportunity to enter the Kingdom was now available to everyone in the preaching of the good news.

Early communities saw the Church as *a new creation, born in the events of Pentecost*. They described the Church as a family, a house or home, a boat, a flock, or a temple. Membership required faith, community, prayer, and acceptance of suffering. More particularly, it required a radical break with previous ways of life, a new direction in life, acceptance of a new, diverse, community, mutual service and appreciation, and constant reconciliation and forgiveness. The new life that resulted from membership in the Church was centered on Christ, based on the Word, and lived in community.

We read that the early Church was a group *living in unity of mind and purpose*. This did not exclude tension among some believers, but the efforts to build up unity were an essential aspect of the faith community. Hospitality epitomized this spirit of community for which believers strove. Missionaries cultivated a spirit of unity in the communities they established, giving the new faithful encouragement and support, helping them set up local community structures, and guiding them in a deeper understanding of the faith. Key to maintaining unity was a deeper understanding of the teachings of the Lord in the Church. Aware of the struggles that communities faced, early writers still described them as united in mind and heart, sharing the teachings of the apostles, community, the breaking of bread, prayer, and their material goods.

So, belonging to the Church and sharing the common life of faith was integral to conversion. The believers' authentic expression of faith was an *ongoing conversion lived out in the heart of the Church*. The communitarian nature of Christian faith was expressed literally and radically in the lifestyle of the primitive Church. It was lived out in tension and suffering, for Christianity was never a single unified vision of life in the Lord. There were several theological currents that existed at the same time, sometimes peacefully, other times not. The Church experienced persecution, but faced internal divisions too. So, the emphasis on unity and sharing was within the context of the normal daily struggles with which most groups of people deal. But the Church was able to discuss its differences and search for common ground in spite of the pain and anguish many felt. Moreover, it does not seem that any of the clashes led to bitterness or resentment.

Church communities were *formed in response to the preaching of the Word of God*. They centered their gathering on the Word proclaimed in the apostles' preaching of the good news. The community's missionaries went forth throughout the world proclaiming the Word of God, and communities came together in response to the Word. The Eucharistic gatherings included readings from the Word, and communities would gather these stories into their regional gospels.

For the early Christians, the Church was neither a place of refuge nor an institution offering ready-made salvation. The Church was *a way of living the communal expression of our faith* and commitment to Christ. There were several key components of the daily life of the early Church communities. We have seen that members of the Church must evidence repentance, belief in Jesus, baptism, and reception of the Spirit. Repentance and change of life were necessary for faith to be authentic. Believers must live in conformity with what the community considered the will of God. Commitment was not a once and for all response but each believer must "remain in the faith." They must show perseverance in faith, an active and dynamic holding fast to the faith, keeping the Word, and doing the Word.

The early communities saw themselves as *a prayerful Church*. The early Church saw Jesus as a model of prayer, and they followed Jesus' example and both communities and individuals became models of prayer. Missionaries taught prayer, communities centered their lives on prayer, and Church leaders considered prayer so important to them that they rearranged ministries and responsibilities in order to give more time to prayer. The picture we see of the praying Church is detailed and highlights prayers of praise, petition, thanksgiving, sorrow, and discernment. The response of the early Church communities was the great challenge to community prayer for Christians of every generation.

While the early Church sustained itself by prayer and worship in their common commitment to the Lord, we also find that the disciples lived as *a truly sharing Church*. We read that they gathered for instruction, common life, the breaking of bread, and prayer. We are told they were of one heart and one mind, took delight in taking their meals together, shared their faith with enthusiasm and joy, and encouraged each other in faith. The depth of their sharing was also seen in the disciples' willingness to share their material goods. They held all things in common, sold their property and goods to share with the needy, and enriched each other with their shared poverty, joy, vision, and mission.

In his own ministry Jesus called people to faith that brings salvation. He called his own Church to renewal through service and ministry. The Church became *a community of service and ministry.* While the primary authority in the Church was the Word of God, the ministry and service of leadership took on importance in the community. The principal ministry of leadership was exercised by the Twelve who lived out their authority collegially, feeling a sense of coresponsibility for the whole Church. Sometimes the community made decisions which the Twelve ratified, sometimes the Twelve made resolutions to which the community consented, and then they kept the faithful informed. The individual apostles played important roles; Peter was the recognized leader and spokesperson, Paul was the great leader of the Gentile mission, sometimes working on his own, sometimes with coworkers. Then there was James, the brother of the Lord, who governed the Jerusalem Church, the seven deacons who helped the needy, and local prophets, teachers, and elders. Then, in addition to the ministry of internal community administration and leadership the missionary was a key minister in the early Church

One of the great forms of community sharing and prayer was *the breaking of bread.* The breaking of bread was an invitation to learn about the Lord and be transformed into Christ. The Word testified to the Lord, but the breaking of bread brought the risen Lord to be with the community. In fact, it emphasized the presence of the Lord in the celebration, and as we saw in the Emmaus story, disciples recognized the risen Jesus in the breaking of bread. So, the breaking of bread was not only an eschatological banquet but the major ritual celebration of the early Church, in which believers shared life, prayer, and community, and in doing so grew in awareness of who Jesus was for them individually and as a people.

We must continue to reflect on the nature of the Church in apostolic times and then make it newly visible in our own times.[12] The Church was *a community which fulfilled peoples' hopes*; a community for our times, a community with a universal vision and a historically important mission, and above all the Church was seen as a community of God. In the Church we are baptized into a new corporate life. We must constantly intensify our awareness of this and live as parts of this ecclesial reality. For us, as for the early Christians, salvation is found in a community based on faith.

Nature of the Church

"I am the vine, you are the branches. He who abides in me, and I in him, he it is that bears much fruit, for apart from me you can do nothing" (Jn 15:5)

The history of the Church has included periods of fidelity to the gospels' vision of what Jesus' community ought to be, as well as times of failure. Nowadays, we have all seen the strengths and weaknesses of life in the Church. After twenty centuries of Church history, Pope Paul VI concluded the Second Vatican Council with the statement, "Now we begin to study the Church." Certainly, after the Council, many of the faithful fostered a deeper awareness and consciousness of what it means to be Church. For a while the leadership of several popes and bishops, was complemented by the growth in ecclesial awareness fostered by spiritual movements, theologians, and outstanding clergy, religious, and laity. The insights and renewal efforts of all these individuals and groups became powerful manifestations of the guidance of the Holy Spirit. They reminded us that more than ever genuine conversion is a conversion to the life of the Church.

The way we understand the Church conditions the way we live as Church. Early New Testament communities had a powerful understanding of what it meant to be Church. History gives us several ways in which people understood the Church, some frighteningly different from Jesus' message. It is common to express our understanding of the Church with the use of images that help give us a moment's intuition into the reality of the Church—maybe, temple, boat, bride, state, crusading army, and so on. Now and again an image helps us form a critical assessment of what it means to be Church and evokes clearly supportive responses among the faithful—institution, community, sacrament, herald, servant, family, and so on. Many faithful have found encouragement and renewed dedication by thinking of the Church as pilgrim people, people of God, chosen assembly, household of the Lord, mystical body of Christ, and so on. While some of these images or models are excellent, others are pastorally impossible to deal with, others provoke polemical reactions, and some are too clerical and exclude most of the baptized. The direction for the future is to find an understanding of the Church that is simple enough to evoke attitudes and courses of action, is clear enough to reflectively and critically deepen our understanding, and is successful in responding to the problems of our time.

When we looked at the New Testament images of Church and the resulting lifestyle, we found a series of challenging components of what they felt was unique about the Church and that needed to be repeated in each successive generation of believers. When we examine these characteristics of the life of the early Church which ones are still essential? And even the ones that are essential do we need to live them in different ways today in order to make them relevant to our own times. Part of learning about faith is to welcome ideas that come through re-learning. Like the guardian of the treasure house in Christian Scripture, we seek to value new things and old ones too.

Three words catch the stages of the process that people pursue in their constant clarification of faith—root, interpret, and discover. We always refer our ideas concerning faith back to the events of Jesus' life and his teachings, and thus we make sure our present understandings are rooted in that experience. That, however, is not enough, for it tells us what the challenges of Christianity were two thousand years ago. We also need to come back to the present, interpreting those teachings for today, otherwise they lose relevance. Since change is so rapid today, we also need to be ever ready to discover new ways to live our spiritual commitment in contemporary situations, both present and future.

Ideas often become obsolete, and articulations of belief systems, including our understanding of the Church, become irrelevant as time passes. When people dedicate themselves to beliefs that are irrelevant it is quite sad and disastrous for them personally. Sometimes we need to change formulations of faith, so that what was formerly spirit and life can become equally challenging in new situations, new generations, and new cultures. We need to make conscious decisions to rethink limiting beliefs and find new ways to express our Christian commitment. This is particularly important when the need for change is left unanswered and gradually deteriorates into a crisis of belief. "Crisis" is a word that means "judgment," and it reminds us that when expressions of belief become progressively irrelevant, there arises the need to bring new ideas to the fore and make different judgments regarding how to articulate Christian values in changed circumstances.

Conversion implies being willing to change. When people cling to a known past, we see the fossilization of beliefs and the emergence of arthritic institutions. But, we need the enrichment that comes with a spirit of discovery. Discovery means leaving behind something and searching for something new. It might be a deeper insight, a refinement of our knowledge, a broadening of our understanding, an awareness of a realm of life beyond this one. In study, reflection, and discussion, we can gain new ideas that keep our commitment relevant, vibrant, and meaningful. These are ways we keep our minds open to be filled with a deeper understanding of faith.

Being Church today

"And I have other sheep, that are not of this fold; I must bring them also; and they will heed my voice. So there shall be one flock, one shepherd" (Jn 10:16)

The Church is in a transition or even in a crisis, at least I hope it is. The thought that the Church could continue in its present form with its current interests and priorities would be depressing. Clearly, the Church has gone through many transitions and crises and has outlived all its critics. However, current losses of members, along with deep dissatisfaction among the faithful, and lack of respect for its leaders and the focus of their teachings have brought the Church to a place where it has not been before. In recent years there have been some swings in emphasis in our understanding of Church. The Church is not only institution but mystery; not only hierarchical but collegial; emphasizes not only office but charism, not only obedience but co-responsibility; not just flight from the world but involvement in it. The resulting tension from different emphases challenges us to ask what is essential in Church communities. The key components of Church life identified by the early Christians led to a community life that was a challenging portrayal of their shared faith. How do we as a contemporary community express our shared faith?

1. *The Church is a community living the call to faith.* Faith is the experience or awareness of the love of God for us all. As a community we appreciate this and thereby see what others do not see and then look at the world in a different way. We are called to help each member to focus on faith and its shared values. We strive to mutually authenticate each other's faith in the love of God, the power of Jesus, and the guidance of the Holy Spirit. We daily become a standard of faith to each other. We work to make sure the focus of the community is not on the organization but on faith.

2. *The Church bases its life on ongoing conversion, symbolized in baptism.* Our commitment immediately calls us to develop a new direction in life, new attitudes, and a new lifestyle. True conversion is the result of faith in Jesus, and it implies turning our backs on previous lifestyles and then journeying towards the Lord. Without conversion there is no authentic presence of the Christian community. In baptism we immerse ourselves in the values and vision of the Lord, and we give ourselves to serve his purposes in the present world. Our Church communities should not be places of comfort in which lives sprinkled with a little religion are approved and sanctioned. They must be places of constant challenge. Whether one is baptized, or nominally a Roman Catholic, or a frequent church-goer is not important. What matters to us is that we be a Church that lives ongoing conversion.

3. *The Church is a community known for its ongoing fidelity to Word and Spirit.* For us as faith-filled people the Bible is a source of inspiration and edification. In it we find a feeling for our faith, a sense of Scripture's priorities, and resonance with disciples of another age. Scripture is also an inspired synthesis and vision of what faith meant to disciples in the early Church. It is a standard for measuring the authenticity of current teachings and practices. The Spirit enables us to interpret the Bible's challenges in meaningful ways for today in the varied situations in which we now find ourselves. It is an occasion for a new proclamation, a norm to evaluate new forms of Church, as it reminds us of the perennially important elements in Jesus' teaching. In it we discover a biblical mentality or perspective which we can live out in new situations, even ones unforeseen by biblical writers. Unfortunately, we often find that not all current priorities of Church leadership reflect the centrality of Word and Spirit. We must firmly insist that they do; participating when they do and withdrawing our support when they do not.

4. *The Church community is a sign and sacrament of unity in faith.* Jesus hoped that his disciples' unity would draw other people to faith. The Church is a community, in the world, to serve the world. When our world is full of division, polarization, hatred, racism, and so on, we, as the Church, must be a different kind of presence—a liberating presence of unity and a loving reconciling presence of God's love. Jesus calls us as Church to model our community life on the union between the Father and Jesus and dedicate ourselves to deepen this union by abiding in God's love. We need to constantly strive for common ground in searching for the essential content of faith and shared ways of living this.

5. *The Church is a community that uses structures and rituals.* The organizational structures and religious rituals should mediate God to the members, and if they do not then they are of

no use. Structures and rituals are expressions of convictions related to faith and must focus on God's ways and not human traditions. We need to approach the various ministries established by the Lord with a sense of shared responsibility that guarantees freedom in responsible involvement and freedom of speech regarding our common vision of Church. Structures and rituals are changeable depending on times and cultures—what is meaningful in one is not in another. We need new forms of structures, of dedicated life, and of priestly ministry, since the ones we have now can often thwart the faith development of many of the faithful. When some people talk about the "church" they actually mean only the administrators who are less than half of one percent of the community. Let us use language carefully; "Church" means all of us.

6. *The Church's common vision must include several essential elements.* Being Church means being a prayerful, sharing, joyful, charismatic, and service centered community. The Church has always recognized the priestly, prophetical, and royal offices of Jesus and committed itself to live these out in contemporary expressions. Thus, we faithful must be prayerful people who live in peace, give ourselves to the service of others, and use all our charisms for the benefit of all. Lives of faith are so satisfying that they lead to the joy that the Lord promised. We must regularly examine our lives to verify that we reflect the essential characteristics of Christian community. We continually find that some Church emphases are distractions, often non-essentials, and fail to help us become the communities for which Jesus hoped. Each of us is responsible for the presentation of the essentials of the Church's life.

7. *The Church community that is essential to faith is both local and universal.* We believe that God offers universal salvation, and that this salvation is received locally in churches all over the world with all their cultural differences. Church is actualized at

both the local and the universal levels. However, local Church is the foundation on which the universal Church is built, and growth takes place primarily at the local level. The universal Church is a communion of local Churches and does not have an existence independent of them. The universal Church best portrays its own identity when it is truly a collegial expression of the life, teachings, and vision of local Churches. While power is generally concentrated in a few top officials, nowadays it is less effective and more frequently questioned. Let us take responsibility for a percolating model of Church.

8. *The Church is above all the community of God.* The Church community lives in the here and now but always with an eye on life beyond this one. We strive to focus our lives on the complete fulfillment of the will of God which has a double focus—love of God and love of neighbor. As people of faith, we appreciate the transcendent in life and realize we are called to be everyday mystics—we live here while being elsewhere. We communicate to others our personal experience of the values of God's vision of promise. We nurture values of the Spirit, listen to the gentle reminders of the Spirit, and are open and receptive to the call of God. We have all become aware that often the Church does not lead us to God. Let us discern which aspects of the Church do and which do not.

The Church is frequently where we find faith and discover ways to nurture it. Disciples who are bound together as the family of the Lord become a standard of faith for each other when faith is under attack. When the Church is at its best it is teacher and guide for those who seek deeper faith. Participating in the life of the Church enriches us with profound understandings of discipleship, educates us to morality and values, and leads us in worship.

Personal reflection

I hope we can all participate in the real and challenging life of the Church as our community way of living our faith. Let us cherish the calling to live our baptismal commitment in ongoing conversion and with fidelity to the Word of God and the inspiration of the Holy Spirit. Let us answer Jesus' call to be a sign to the world of the unity God wants for all people. Let us utilize structures and rituals in service to faith and constantly focus on what is central to the nature of the Church. May we work at being God's community locally and universally, presenting ourselves to all as a sacrament of salvation.

Questions for discussion or personal reflection

1. How would you describe the Church?

2. Give specific examples of how you participate in the life of the Church.

3. If you could not participate in the life of the Church what would you miss?

Chapter Fourteen

DISCOVERING THE ENERGIES OF FAITH

As people dedicated to spiritual growth we need to know our own inner strengths and energies and use them effectively to maintain our own value systems and to positively impact our surrounding environment. Some of us will have different strengths than others, and we can complement each other in our communities of faith. But there are some common forces for good that can energize us all and can help us nurture our faith.[13]

Develop a sense of call

Each of us needs to rediscover our call in life and faithfully pursue it with fortitude. The core values that motivate our lives give rise to an awareness of our enduring purpose in life. In other words we see things that we can do well and that seem to consistently do good to others. The good that we consistently do because of the gifts we have becomes part of our mission in life.

We can deepen this awareness of what we can do well for the common good and make it a firmly established part of our lives. We feel called to respond in ways we know affect others and our environment positively. This sense of call points us to our own destiny in life. It cannot be sporadic or episodic, but it needs to be a deliberate part of our self-concept. Knowing we have a calling energizes us and intensifies the good we can do. We arrive at a point where we cannot ignore this drive for goodness within ourselves; rather we are unable to do anything but intensify it. It is a vocation, and the personal integrity of each of us relates to us faithfully following this call.

Feeling we are in this world for a reason is a spiritual awakening, and once we identify it then this sense of call develops an internal dynamic of its own. It grows within us, clarifying this important aspect of our personalities. Faithfully following our call is an inward journey of self-discovery, a life-changing journey during which we find our role in the plan of God. Few aspects of life energize us more than knowing we can never be our true selves without faithfully pursuing this call.

When we become aware of our own calling, we also see ourselves within a larger context. Call in this world has no meaning outside an awareness of another realm of life. Thus, a sense of call relates directly to our spiritual growth and faith. When we confront ourselves in the larger context of the meaning of life, we see ourselves more clearly than at any other time. We cannot make excuses or decide we do not wish to respond. In the experience we see ourselves immediately in relationship to God and see ourselves exactly as we are, with our strengths and our gifts, and immediately know that we have a calling that we must pursue.

Discern before deciding

Life is complicated, and we are constantly faced with making decisions that reflect the values of our faith-filled experiences and spiritual commitment. At every turn in life we must choose freely between various alternatives. Nowadays, there are no easy answers; situations change rapidly, authorities do not have pre-packaged answers like they used to, and the "right" response is not always evident. We make choices with humility, knowing we will often be wrong. However, with humility and courage we must choose, for to refuse to make a decision that reflects our values is itself a decision with serious implications.

Discernment is an inner energy by which we assess alternatives in light of our spiritual commitments. It is a self-training to make judgments based on values that we want to guide our lives. It is not haphazard but a specific method of reflecting, assessing alternatives, clarifying implications of decisions, and opening our hearts to the guidance of the Holy Spirit. At first it takes significant time, but with practice we can do it very speedily, almost intuitively. This critical analysis of alternatives is a judgment made in light of our faith-filled vision of life. It is an exercise of wisdom. Too many people do not think enough before making decisions and so do not deliberately impact their environment with their values.

Discernment requires honesty, openness, and prayerfulness. It also calls for flexibility, foresight, and creativity. It means being a good listener—to self, others, the world, the signs of the times, the hopes of humanity, and the cries of the needy and suffering. Judgments need to be based on what we discern to be the best thing to do in any given situation, and to do that effectively we must be open to the signs of goodness, justice, and love, and sensitive to cries against evil, injustice, and hatred. Then, in light of our values we can choose which alternative is best and make judgments accordingly.

Discernment is an energy of the spirit. When practiced consistently it helps us live intentionally and deliberately in light of the values of our faith-filled experiences. It can gradually transform our lives, focusing them in ways that help us become who we want to be and to be known for the values for which we want to be known. Were discernment a major theme and practice in our local churches it would be a huge plus in the life and mission of the Church.

Be single-minded

A particularly significant energy of the spirit that furthers commitment to a depth of spiritual dedication is single-mindedness. This attitude is mentioned in the Bible as a beatitude: "Blessed are the pure in heart, for they will see God" (Mt 5:8). So, we are talking about an uncontaminated pursuit of the values that guide our lives. In the Bible, heart is as much the source of knowledge and conviction as it is of love. Single-mindedness or single-heartedness focuses on implementing values. It is the relentless pursuit of integrity, making sure our lives always reflect the values of our inner spirit.

Single-mindedness refers to clarity of purpose in life, a daily determination to be faithful to values that motivate us. We always need to complement this energy of the spirit with humility. Because we are determined about something does not mean we are always right. After all, there are many world leaders, national leaders, and maybe even friends of ours who confuse stubbornness and arrogance with the single-minded pursuit of values. Rather, we need to pursue our values with humility, listening to the challenges of others, purifying when necessary. Change and effort to refocus preserve the uniqueness of the values we pursue.

We live in a complex world where people have different value systems. Some values we will hold in common, but others no. Our single-minded pursuit of motivating values is always within the context of other good people's pursuit of their value systems. So, single-mindedness is lived out with courageous determination and also with mutual respect for innumerable differences resulting from history, culture, religious traditions, and so on.

For each of us, single-mindedness is an energy of the spirit that manifests the depth of awareness of our call and of the conviction that comes through discernment. It shows forth our integrity, the balance between what we experience and how we live following that experience. The Bible says such people "will see God"; the single-minded pursuit of values that result from faith helps each of us to transcend self-interest and opens each of us to perceive the call of God.

Practice patient-urgency

The strategy of firing up the energies of the spirit must include the double quality of patient-urgency. We must have patience in living faithfully those values that motivate us in the transformation of ourselves and of our world. However, we cannot be too patient! It is important, even urgent, that we bring about change. Patience will be required for the work is difficult. Too much patience thwarts the attaining of our goal. It is urgent that the work of transformation proceed. Too much urgency can hinder the calm, gradual transformation that is needed and can alienate others who need to be part of the transformation. So, an important energy of the spirit is the double quality of patient-urgency.

We need patient-urgency in coping with the normal pressures of everyday life. This takes patience but we cannot neglect the urgency to bring values to our world. In the Sermon on the Mount Jesus declares, "Blessed are those who mourn, for they shall be comforted," and "Blessed are the meek, for they will inherit the earth" (Mt 5:4-5). These are both strong qualities, both part of the patient-urgency we need. The former refers to those who undergo life's hardships and live patiently through oppression, domination, and abuse of their rights, while striving to be faithful to their values. The latter refers to those who accept life under God without complaint. These dedicated individuals strive with urgent commitment to respond to their calling while patiently enduring the problems such fidelity brings. Such individuals are in tune with their essential calling and remain committed to it in spite of the domination of evil around them. Patient-urgency is a prophetical stance in a world that often loses values that matter.

It is, of course, urgent that as people of faith we have a clearly focused impact on our world. Left to ourselves we can drift into mediocrity and then into periods without the values we had felt called to uphold. Our world easily slides into situations where evil seems more dominant than goodness. Our faith-filled experiences of God's loving challenge call us to dedicate ourselves to our own and to the world's transformation. We are challenged to build lives anew on values that help us be the best we are capable of being. It is urgent that this transformation progress. So, we need to live daily, motivated by a sense of patient-urgency.

Enjoy life

As people of faith, we should be naturally optimistic and enthusiastic about our lives, and convinced that they be full of joy. Unfortunately, some people find their joy in personal pleasure and self-satisfaction or in a sense of achievement beyond that of others around them. We find joy and happiness in making a difference to our own and to other people's lives and in giving ourselves to the appreciation of values beyond the normal horizons of life. We should enjoy doing good, being good, and experiencing ultimate goodness.

We find joy and delight in the ordinary events of life. We can be fully present to people and to events, appreciating them and enjoying them as gifts that they are to us from a gracious God. Our faith gives us a new perspective on life. Sharing is more important to us than competition with others. We can delight in others' achievements rather than comparing them to our own. We value the contributions of everyone and reject the typical mutual blame found in so much of contemporary society. A positive outlook with optimism and enthusiasm brings about joy. People of faith should enjoy life.

When we are filled with joy we are also peacemakers, and that is one of the reasons why this energy of the spirit is so important. In a world of hatred, polarization, discrimination, and deliberate hurt, we, as people energized by joy, can bring about peacefulness in ourselves, in others around us, and in that part of society we can influence. Having stretched beyond the normal horizons of life we encountered a vision of the human community living in love and peace, and we now daily strive to make that hope a reality.

We meet many people who always seem burdened with problems that life brings them, or with themselves and their poor self-concept, or with others' lack of respect for them, and so on. So much of our experience is of a joyless world, but we have a mission to spread joy. It is an energy of our spirit.

Be generous

Every experience in our spiritual lives is an experience of God's generosity towards us, reminding us that we must live with generosity towards others. Generosity implies treating others with goodness, abundant support, and prodigious gestures of loving service. When we are generous, we move the focus away from ourselves to emphasize the importance of others.

Generosity can sometimes appropriately refer to financial support for the needy, those who a have suffered from natural disasters, the homeless, and the unemployed. This practical way of helping those in need is a fine quality of good human beings everywhere. However, generosity is essentially about self-gift, sharing with others our time when they need it; our words to support, encourage, console, and motivate; our presence to people in compassionate care, understanding, and love; our forgiveness to those who may have done us harm. Generosity means giving not taking. It is a gesture from those who have to those who have not, provided we always appreciate that generosity is mutual. We are all always the haves and have nots at the same time, for those who give receive by their giving.

Generosity is an energy of our inner spirit and is part of who we are. We evidence it in all situations. Thus, we live generously with close friends and family, as much as with strangers, coworkers, and the needy. We show friends and family love without measure. In dealing with them we strive to choose the most loving thing to do, to forgive abundantly, to show limitless understanding, and to be magnanimous in our relationships. As we live with generosity, we are daily becoming who we are capable of being, for generosity is creative of our personalities.

This energy of the spirit leads us to have a benevolent attitude to all. We learn to wish others well even before we know them. This anticipatory benevolence towards all, based as it is on our experience of God's approach toward us, contributes towards mutual understanding and respect, dialogue, collaboration, and community building. Generosity is a wonderful energy of the human spirit and should not be left to chance or show itself only sporadically. We need to deliberately channel this quality.

Show compassion

Compassion is one of the most beautiful qualities that we can extend to others. If we train ourselves to make this an intentional response, we draw out an energy of the spirit that can transform society. Compassion means "to suffer with," and it describes being with others in the intimacy of their pain. Compassion means feeling the way others do in their suffering, enduring the pain with them, and supporting them in mutual efforts. Compassion is a healing service to others, journeying with them through the difficulties of their lives.

Our contemporary world is no different than it has been in other times, it gives little evidence of compassion. Rather, it is often characterized by selfishness, greed, and abuse of others. So many seem to choose dominant, hateful approaches to others.

When we show compassion, the evil of this world cannot deal with it. They certainly cannot oppose it for it is clearly a genuine quality, at the heart of humanity. In fact, evil people in our world do not know what to do with compassion. They see it, silently appreciate it, sometimes mock it as weakness, but can never oppose it.

We show compassion to ourselves and our failures, to others in their many needs, to the world when the environment is abused. There is so much pain, loss, sickness, and abuse. People are marginalized and discriminated against for all kinds of reasons. Our compassion needs to be practical and implies fighting for justice. Ours has to be more than a believed-in compassion, it has to be real. This will imply not being afraid to show our feelings and emotions as we suffer together with those in pain. We also need to identify the causes of pain, to seek alleviation in the short term where possible, and to pursue solutions for situations that bring so much torment and suffering.

Sometimes there are no solutions to the pain people feel. It might be a terminal illness that has no end except further pain and death. It could be the loss of loved ones through sickness or in an accident, or tragically taken in war, or in a natural disaster. There is really nothing we can do. God does not act in the way human beings think God should act. We need to be together in mutual compassion faced with a mystery we do not understand, trusting in God's love that we cannot see, believing in a divine plan we cannot understand. We strive to be together, to console each other, to sustain each other's commitment, and to let each other know our love.

Live in touch with tradition

A spiritual experience of people of faith always includes a sense of community, for in the transforming experience one sees a realm beyond this one that portrays God's plan for the world—a plan for salvation in a loving community. But we also see our experience as a point in history, and know we belong to a tradition of God's love and of the human struggle to respond. This awareness that we are a part of a community and that we stand at a point in history with a past and a future can energize us in our responses to the challenges of spiritual growth.

We have a history, we have connections with ancestors who have lived, loved, survived, and grown, and we can appreciate them as models to be imitated and sometimes to be avoided. Some were ordinary figures and others even heroic. They are an integral part of our own lives. There are also those who will come into existence in the future and who are already linked to us. We look in both directions and sense our responsibility for our vision of life, linked to the past and maybe creative of the future.

Our connections are not only with family members but with humanity in its struggles to solve the most fundamental questions concerning the meaning of life. We learn what it means to be human and pass our awareness on to others. We welcome the great figures of our past, saints and mystics, who teach, inspire, motivate, and enlighten us on our current pursuit of the journey they already took. Certainly we are part of a communion of humanity; call it a communion of saints if you wish. Living aware of this need to maintain traditions draws out values of the spirit in our contemporary struggles.

In this context, community expressions of faith in God can support, nurture, and strengthen our dedication. Belief systems formulated by others can help, even though they cannot substitute for our personal experiences of faith. Even religions with their awkwardness and graciousness, with their frequent corruption and constant challenge, with their sporadic causes and perennial standards—such communities can help us, as we become integral parts of a community of shared faith. Preserving a sense of tradition can be a fruitful energy of our spirit.

Faith is a gift of God that transforms us in every aspect of our lives. Faith includes many concrete attitudes to life that manifest the values that result from faith. These become energies of our souls, opportunities to share in the wondrous gifts of God. To be a person of faith means to be particularly blest by God. These energies are gifts that God entrusts to us to develop for the benefit of others.

Personal reflection

At times we see gifts in ourselves and in others and we appreciate how God has blessed us. Often we use these gifts and often we waste them. Let us strive to use these energies of our inner spirits to grow in faith and be grateful for the faith we have.

Questions for discussion or personal reflection

1. Which of these energies of faith are part of your life?

2. Do you thank God for the spiritual gifts that you have?

3. Have you noticed these gifts in your family or friends?

Chapter Fifteen

CENTERING OUR LIVES ON JESUS CHRIST

Who was Jesus Christ?

"And Jesus returned in the power of the Spirit into Galilee, a report concerning him went out through all the surrounding country. And he taught in their synagogues being glorified by all" (Lk 4:14)

Jesus Christ had simple origins. He was born in Nazareth, the son of a carpenter, Joseph, and his young wife, Mary. He was well known locally, as were his close relatives. His life was withdrawn, and he unknown until he was around thirty years old. Jesus was from Galilee, whose people were more open-minded than the Judeans. The latter were scrupulously law-abiding, and their leaders, at times, narrow-minded. Jesus, on the other hand, loved the Law, but was not enslaved to legalistic interpretations of it, but showed always that people's needs came first.

When he was around thirty years old, Jesus began to travel around the towns and villages of Galilee with an awareness that he was to preach to the people and call them to change the direction of their lives. He came across as being very human, showing ignorance of some events, and demonstrating strong emotions; he was moved with pity at others' sufferings, delighted to be in the company of little children, was appreciative of others' dedication, and grieved at other people's close-mindedness. He was angry with some in his audience, grieved when he met with rejection, and indignant when his wishes were thwarted. Towards the end of his ministry he was filled with fear, sorrow, and distress. Throughout his life he often showed how deeply he felt the need to pray personally, through ritual, and in times of pain and confrontation.

Jesus' public ministry lasted for only three years and was limited to a very small region between Galilee and Jerusalem, about eighty five miles. When we first hear of him, he was already preaching persuasively and with authority about God's new kingdom on earth, calling everyone to repentance, and claiming that his own presence was reason for rejoicing. His ministry was well received and his reputation as a powerful teacher spread throughout the surrounding region of Galilee. At first he was recognized preeminently as a teacher who spoke on his own authority, unlike the Jewish leaders of his time who spoke within the authority of the group based in the official synagogue and canonical texts. A rich young man addressed Jesus as "good teacher," and his disciples, strangers, Pharisees, Herodians, Sadducees, and scribes, all addressed Jesus as "teacher."

A particular characteristic of Jesus' life was the suffering he faced to remain faithful to his message and to what he saw as God's calling to preach the "good news." He had to face opposition from religious authorities who accused him of blasphemy and plotted to kill him. He had to deal with misunderstanding from his family and disciples. He suffered especially from a realization that greater suffering lay ahead that provoked a crescendo of fear and distress. So, Jesus' ministry brought rejection from all sides, blindness to the nature of his life and work, malicious plotting by opponents, slanderous accusations against his ministry, fearful foreboding, and a general abandonment of Jesus to a lonely acceptance of his destiny. Finally, Jesus was abandoned in death; forsaken, rejected, betrayed, mocked, scourged, and crucified. However, a consistent belief of the Christian communities was that Jesus rose from the dead and became the object of their faith. Considering his origins, it is remarkable that the early Church communities thought of Jesus as so special. This was clearly their experience.

The early Church wrote down its memories and understandings of the nature and meaning of Jesus' life and ministry in a collection of gospels written from around the years 65 to 90, and these were preceded by a series of apostolic letters written as early as the year 51 and after. So, within thirty years of Jesus' death the early Church had formulated strong beliefs about who Jesus was and especially who he was, and now is, for his followers. They stressed that all that Jesus did was in fidelity to his Father's will and in continuity with God's plan for the salvation of humankind. Jesus was seen as re-living the history of the Chosen People—he started in the waters of transformation, went out to the desert, and then climbed a mountain to receive God's teachings. Twice we are told the voice of God declared Jesus as his Son in whom he was well pleased. Jesus was seen as the presence of the Father, in fact, as the Son of God. The gospel writers gathered the teachings of Jesus and showed us how powerful his message was. Jesus fulfilled the hopes of the Chosen People, and now fulfills our hopes too. He had a mission to save people from sin, and now heals all our ills too. Many people acknowledged him as a great teacher, and now he teaches us all about life. The fact that Jesus knows the Father and reveals him to us indicates his mediational role, and now he binds us to each other, as he gathers us together and calls for reconciliation, benevolence, love, and forgiveness. Jesus is especially our Lord. Lord is a title that conveys awe resulting from the awareness that the many ways of designating Jesus are all facets of the same transcending person. And now, Jesus is our Lord and judge.

The early Christian community, spurred on by their convictions that Jesus was different, quickly gathered together the teachings of Jesus in individual sayings and great sermons, and they complemented these with episodes in his life that showed his power in miracles and his attitudes to others in stories of concern, compassion, and challenge. They saw Jesus as loyal to his Father, committed to his mission, sensitive to people's hopes and needs, a prophetical challenge to a sinful world, and constantly aware of who he must be for the service and salvation of others. They saw Jesus' baptism by John as a new creation story and his coming as the beginning of a new phase in human history. His coming signified the fulfillment of God's promises that a special anointed one, or Messiah, would bring about world transformation in a new kingdom of God on earth. They believed Jesus to be the Son of God, the Servant of the Lord, the Bestower of the Spirit, and the Savior of the world. They called him Lord, the Righteous One, the Instrument of God's designs, and above all the object of their faith—all within thirty years of Jesus' death.

When the community looked back over the life and teachings of Jesus they concluded that they had seen the glory of God in Jesus. He was the Word of God who became flesh, the pre-existent Lord who was with God and was God, he was sent by the Father as revealer of the Father's teachings and as the light of the world. They acknowledged in faith a lasting relationship of love between Father and Son; "The Father is in me, and I am in the

Father." The apostle Thomas sums up the belief of the early Church when he says about Jesus, "you are my Lord and my God." So, for the early Christians the presence of Jesus, his life and mission, was nothing less than the irruption of the divine in human history, and they believed that this experience was not just for people of Jesus' own time but for the whole world. While different communities emphasized different understandings of Jesus, common features of faith are present in them all.

Jesus' life represents the beginning of a new era of God's creative interventions in the world. Jesus is the sign and sacrament of God's compassion and love. He is the Suffering Servant of the Lord, who through his life and death becomes the living Lord of all. Now he remains present to his Church in signs and wonders, in the power of his name, in the reconciling ministry of the Church, and in the examples of his disciples.[14]

Jesus Christ is the object of our faith

"Now when Jesus came into the district of Caesarea Philippi, he asked his disciples 'Who do men say that the Son of man is?'. . .
He said to them, 'But who do you say that I am?'" (Mt 16:13, 15)

On the occasion of a visit by Jesus and the apostles to a town called Caesarea Philippi, Jesus took time to ask the apostles who people thought he was and they gave various answers. However, Jesus was more interested in asking them "But who do you say that I am" (Mt 16:15). Peter answered "You are the Christ, the Son of the living God" (Mt 16:16). Later, when the writer of the *Acts of Apostles* describes Peter's decision to find a substitute apostle for the betrayer Judas, he insisted it had to be someone who had personal experience of Jesus, "beginning with the baptism of John until the day he was taken up from us" (Acts 1:22). The question, "who do you say Jesus is," is the fundamental question that continues to face every individual Christian as well as the entire Church. The answer must be based on personal experience of Jesus. It is not a proof, it is faith. Statements of belief will follow, and so too will the organization of the Church, but first comes a personal relationship of faith. The disciples who travelled with Jesus and saw who he was and what he did were clearly convinced that he was so special they gave him several titles that expressed who they believed him to be. This growing awareness continued in the evolution of Christology especially in the early Church.

Faith seeks understanding as we have already seen in the development of the gospels and what they thought about Jesus. At first, the focus was on Jesus as Word (Logos) and reflected on his pre-existence. This continued in the early post-apostolic Church and then in a series of ecumenical councils that wrestled with the nature of Jesus—was he human or divine or both, what was Jesus' relationship to the Father and to the Holy Spirit, was Mary the mother of a man or of God, did Jesus die on the cross as man or as God, was the resurrection real or a statement of faith. The first seven ecumenical councils—gatherings of representatives from Churches all over the world—struggled with these and other issues relating to Jesus and formulated their convictions in creeds that expressed beliefs. At times these were influenced by different philosophical positions of East and West, and at times by the interference of emperors. Later, in the middle ages, reflections stressed Jesus as judge and gave rise to an emphasis on fear, sin, sacrifice, atonement, and final judgment. At the same time spiritual writers and mystics emphasized Jesus' humanity and stressed imitation, friendship, spiritual marriage, and love. Nowadays, the question "who do you say that I am" draws answers from different groups in their search and has given rise to Jesus' role in liberational, feminist, black, and other groups and their theologies.

The Church's discussions and formulations of creeds and doctrines have been an integral part of the struggle to clarify common elements of shared beliefs and practices. Faithful followers of Jesus in the Church recite these collections of doctrines and commit themselves to believe them. They contain profound statements written by theologians, often as the result of debates in ecumenical councils, and they are not easily understood by those followers who recite them. Even after these important aspects of Church beliefs, the fundamental question raised by Jesus is still the same, "But who do you say that I am." Let us look at some common elements that form the basis of our faith.

1. *Jesus comes from God and reveals who God is.* God is "Sovereign Lord," "Most High God," who is mighty, holy, strong, a God of glory, the living God, creator of heaven and earth, and the omnipotent director of world history. To this image of God as Sovereign Lord Jesus added two unusual features in his revelation of God. First, God is also our Father who is merciful towards us, helps us in our needs, protects us from danger, and treats all equally with no partiality. As Father, he loves the world, takes away the sin of the world, and gave his only Son for the salvation of the world. Second, God has a plan for us and for the whole world. God determines, ordains, and fixes the events of world development and the saving events of Jesus' life. Jesus lives in complete conformity to this plan and executes it for the Father. This plan includes the life, death, and exaltation of Jesus. So, our response as disciples to this image of God is awe, wonder, reverential fear, and adoration. At the same time we can respond with confidence because of God's merciful concerns for us all.

2. Jesus reveals God's life as a threefold mystery of Father, Son, and Holy Spirit. Jesus refers to the activities of Father, Son, and Spirit, frequently presenting them as having distinct functions and often as having the same. He speaks of them as three personal aspects of one God. The Father is the source of life, is all-powerful, has a plan for the world, and is motivated by love in all that he does. Jesus is the instrument of the Father's designs, his teachings are not his own but the Father's, and he and the Father are one. The Holy Spirit is the source of inspiration in the Scriptures and in the teachings of the prophets. The Holy Spirit is from the Father and signals that the times of waiting are over. Jesus is filled with the Spirit and anointed by the Spirit. In fact, Jesus is so full of the spirit that he becomes the source of the Spirit for us all. The Spirit gives birth to the Church and inspires and directs it. He is the promise of the Father and the Spirit of Jesus who continues to guide the Church by reminding them of Jesus' teachings. God does not ration his Spirit who dwells in the hearts of believers as a new presence of Jesus. So, our response is awe before this unique revelation of God.

3. Jesus embodies the presence of God. Jesus has a personal relationship with God. He tells us that his teachings are the Father's and his powerful works are done by the Father, and he wants the works of God to be made visible through him. In fact, the Father loves the Son, sent the Son into the world, and has given over everything to the Son. Jesus is the only Son, always present at the Father's side, and shares a deep union with the Father: "The Father and I are one" (Jn 10:30). Jesus embodies the fullness of the divinity and so can say "Whoever has seen me has seen the Father" (Jn 14:9). Early disciples were so convinced of this that they believed with all their hearts that Jesus was God's presence on earth.

4. Jesus fulfills the Father's will in perfect obedience. At every moment in his life and ministry Jesus, the obedient Servant of the Lord, calls his disciples to imitate his obedience to the will of the Father, insisting that this very obedience makes us his disciples. The Father, who wills that none be lost, constantly guides and shepherds his people. His call is fatherly, his hopes are compassionate, and his love is perfect. When disciples respond to the Father by obedience to his will, they enter into joy. When they refuse, they impose upon themselves an alienation described as judgment. The will of the Father now comes to us in Jesus.

5. Jesus reveals who we are and who we are called to become. He clearly has a loving solidarity with all men and women. Jesus indicates that he wants a special relationship between himself and those who believe in him. He wants to be always in their company so they can share special experiences and teachings. His call implies a personal and unique response from followers that includes commitment, obedience, mission, and witness. Disciples grow in their appreciation of their own life and mission as a result of their closeness to Jesus, and they develop a deeper understanding of who they are called to become. They not only make a personal commitment to Jesus—their hope, healer, teacher, unifier, mediator, and Lord, but the Lord challenges them to intensify their dedication to the fellowship they experience among themselves—in humility, vigilance, compassion, obedience, and community responsibility. No one can earn the call from Jesus. He chooses who he wants, the initiative is always his, and he knows what he wants for each of us.

6. Jesus calls those who have faith in him to change the direction of their lives. Jesus challenges his followers to take a new direction in life centered on him, and he offers them a new comprehensive way of looking at life. To those who seek life with him he says "Come to me . . . I will refresh you. Take my yoke . . .

learn from me. Your souls will find rest" (Mt 11:28-30). This commitment has two steps; reform your life, turning away from former values and launching in a new direction that includes obedience to his teachings, inner sincerity, and detachment from anything that might diminish the exclusiveness of Jesus' claim to our commitment. This repentance and reform leads to faith. It includes four components. Conversion is always to the person Jesus and not to a list of teachings. It starts with an awareness of sin and the need of healing. It is stimulated by the realization that the all-powerful God is actively interested and involved in our lives. It happens when we are also aware that the Lord to whom we are called will return as universal judge. The end of this process is Jesus' hope that his followers will remain in his love.

7. *Jesus teaches us new attitudes to life.* The great sermons of Jesus provide people of faith with the new attitudes to life that ought to be theirs as a result of their commitment to the Lord. Those who live these new approaches to life will be happy and will become salt and light for the whole world. Along with these new attitudes they will need new approaches to religious practices, to laws, and to authenticity in religious devotions. Jesus wants disciples who are spiritually poor, can face life's hardships, who accept life under God without complaint, hunger and thirst for holiness, are compassionate, single-minded and single-hearted, are peacemakers, and can endure persecution to be faithful to the Lord's call. Jesus does not want minimalistic approaches to commands against murder, adultery, divorce, oath-taking, retaliation, and restrictive love. Rather, he seeks to give voice to everyone, and he wants reconciliation, respect for women, growth in human relationships, truthfulness and authenticity, peace and compassion, and universal love.

8. *Jesus asks that each of us form a personal relationship with him.* Discipleship means imitation of Jesus, being ready to always

follow his way of life, accepting his cross, proclaiming his message in service to the world. Disciples are blessed with the privilege of Jesus' constant presence and company. From this there results a deep relationship with God, with others in the Church, with the world, and a transformation of their entire lives. Jesus is the good shepherd who knows each one personally. Disciples are his own friends to whom he entrusts all that he is and has, and his self-gift actually makes them who they are. The union between the Father and Jesus is the model for the disciples' union with Jesus, and the life of the disciple is an ongoing deepening of this union: "Remain in me, as I remain in you. . . . Remain in my love" (Jn 15: 4, 9).

9. *Jesus offers a platform for justice and reform.* Jesus comes to bring his Father's word, and this includes condemning unjust social conditions and challenging society's values. For Jesus there is a close link between discipleship and commitment to social reform, and the absence of concrete efforts to justice jeopardizes repentance and response to the Lord's call. Jesus ministered to the underprivileged, the poor, the oppressed, and the outcasts of society. His example shows us that faith goes beyond religious renewal and includes a new model for society, a politics of challenging the status of the privileged class, of empowering others, of breaking social boundaries, and of transforming society to reflect the values of God's message.

10. *Jesus prepares us for life beyond this one.* We call Jesus "Lord," a title that expresses reverence, majesty, and judgment. He often refers to himself as "Son of Man," a title based on the image of the final judge. Jesus' authority extends to the final judgment when "all the nations will be assembled before him" (Mt 25:32), and he will judge evildoers and reward his faithful disciples who have built their lives on his word and who welcome his coming in glory (Mt 23:39). From the very first call, conversion is always in the perspective of judgment. Those who are "his own" reject darkness,

the world, evil, and unbelief. But others belong to this world and do not speak the truth, and some even among those who have received the message still slip away. Jesus insisted, "I came into this world for judgment" (Jn 9:39). Again Jesus says, "Those who have done good deeds (come forth) to the resurrection of life, but those who have done wicked deeds to the resurrection of condemnation" (Jn 5:29).Those who have been faithful to Jesus look forward to judgment with joy.

Our faith is based on the revelations of Jesus Christ. In giving ourselves to learn from Jesus we are fostering our faith. A key concept of this book is that faith is not a series of abstract teachings that we intellectually accept, it is a relationship with a person, Jesus Christ. Jesus has a personal relationship with God and reveals to us who God is. He fulfills the will of God in every aspect of his life and teaches us to do the same. He calls us to faith, teaches us, and challenges us to make the changes in life that faith requires. Our faith calls us to imitate Jesus in every aspect of our lives.

Personal reflection

When I think of Jesus' life and ministry I am always shocked to see how short it was and how restricted it was in the area and people he dealt with. Within a short time Jesus was known by people all over the Mediterranean region and beyond. His message spread rapidly, and people everywhere dedicated their lives to follow his teachings and accept him as the object of their faith. As people of faith, we must constantly remind ourselves of Jesus' question, "But who do you say that I am." Then we must also ask ourselves how we will live because of our answer.

Questions for discussion or personal reflection

1. How would you answer Jesus' question, "Who do you say that I am?

2. Why do you call yourself a Christian?

3. Which aspects of Jesus' life impress you the most?

POSTSCRIPT

We have looked at some of the struggles we all face in our contemporary search for meaning in life and for God. We live in times that are not among the greatest in the history of religion and in the relevance of the Church. We must maturely and honestly face up to these problems and struggles, otherwise our dedication in faith will become artificial and will not be a real faith-filled response to God's call and challenge in our contemporary world. We may need to live in the midst of some of these problems without hope of immediate change. We may react and respond to others motivated by faith, with a desire to make our commitment more authentic by removing abuse and failures. It is harder to believe than it used to be but our responsibility is clear—our response must be courageous and firm.

We have searched for reasons to believe and there are many. We have looked carefully at our lives and our world and explicitly identified signs of God's presence and power. Some traces of God's love will be the same we have always recognized, and others will be new. We must make explicit in faith what was only implicit, uncover what has been lost, and discover new reasons to deepen our faith.

Our faith development is nourished by our own lives of dedication to spiritual growth, prayer, community growth, energies of faith, and above all by centering our lives on Jesus Christ, the source of faith. We know we have often not given these aspects of our dedication sufficient effort nor prepared ourselves adequately to receive God's gifts. Let us recommit ourselves to the sources of our life of faith.

May our faith mature, expand, and deepen. This is our hope.

ENDNOTES

1. See the Italian newspaper, *La Repubblica 16/01/18*, p.7.
2. For documentation of this section see the Pope's recent Christmas messages to the Curia, especially 2014-2017.
3. For further reading on this section see the following books. The authors have been criticized but their documentation is hard to deny. Gianluigi Nuzzi, *Merchants in the Temple: Inside Pope Francis' Secret Battle Against Corruption in the Vatican*, New York, NY: Henry Holt and Co., 2015; *Via Crucis*, 2017; Emiliano Fittipaldi, *Avarice*, 2013; *Luxury*, 2017.
4. For further reading see Gianluigi Nuzzi, *Original Sin*, 2017.
5. The references in the text are taken from the book by J. B. Metz, *The Emergent Church: The Future of Christianity in a Postbourgeois World*, New York: Crossroad Publishing Co., 1981; the page references given in this section are from this book.
6. For further ideas for this section see Johann Baptist Metz, *The Emergent Church*, chapter two, pp.1-16, and John K. Downey, "Political Theology and Francis of Assisi," p. 191, in *Finding Saint Francis in Literature and Art*, Cynthia Ho, Beth A. Mulvaney, and John K. Downey, eds. New York: Palgrave Macmillan, 2009, pp. 183-201.

7. See Metz, and Downey, and the article in *Civita Cattolica* by Antonio Spadaro and Marceo Figueroa, *http://www.laciviltacattolica.it/articolo/evangelical-fundamentalism-and-catholic-integralism-in-the-usa-a-surprising-ecumenism.*

8. For more details on this section, see my book, *Rediscovering Jesus' Priorities, 2013.*

9. For more detailed development of ideas in this chapter on hope see the first chapter in my book, *Courageous Hope,* New York/Mahwah, NJ: Paulist Press, 2011.

10. For further reading on the material of this section, see my book, *The One Thing Necessary: The Transforming Power of Christian Love,* Chicago: Acta Publications, 2012, especially the chapter on "Love's Vision."

11. This chapter is based on ideas presented in chapter nine of my book, *The Contemporary Challenge of St. Teresa of Avila,* 2016.

12. For detailed comments on the nature of the Church in the New Testament, with detailed references, see my collection of commentaries on the *Gospels* and *Acts* (Biblical Spirituality and Everyday Life) published by wipfandstock.com.

13. This chapter is taken from my book, *Ten Strategies to Nurture Our Spiritual Lives,* 2013, chapter four.

14. For a more detailed presentation of the portraits of Jesus in the gospels, see my collection of commentaries on the *Gospels* and *Acts* (Biblical Spirituality and Everyday Life) published by wipfandstock.com.

Other books of interest

CONTEMPORARY SPIRITUALITY FOR CHRISTIAN ADULTS

This current book is volume 3 in a series of books on contemporary spirituality of Christian adults. A new spirit is stirring in the Church. We must overcome the failures of the past and prepare ourselves for a future of growth and responsibility. Let us rekindle spiritual insight, accept our spiritual destiny, and refocus on the essential teaching of salvation. While many have left the institutional churches, and sadly may never return, perhaps the challenge to renewal of Pope Francis may re-attract them to the essentials of Christian commitment. The Church will grow and benefit from an informed laity who deepens knowledge of the essential teachings of faith. I wrote these books, targeting areas of personal reflection valuable for individuals and discussion groups for this purpose.

Ten Strategies to Nurture Our Spiritual Lives: Don't stand still—nurture the life within you.

This book is volume I in the series CONTEMPORARY SPIRITUALITY FOR CHRISTIAN ADULTS. It presents ten key steps or strategies to support and express the faith of those individuals who seek to deepen their spirituality through personal commitment and group growth. These ten key components of spirituality enable dedicated adults to bring out the meaning of their faith and to facilitate their spiritual growth. It offers a program of reflection, discussion, planning, journaling, strategizing, and sharing.

Rediscovering Jesus' Priorities.

This book, volume 2 in the series CONTEMPORARY SPIRITUALITY FOR CHRISTIAN ADULTS, urges readers to look again at Jesus' teachings and identify the major priorities. It is a call to rethink the essential components of a living and vital Christianity and a challenge to rediscover the basic values Jesus proclaimed. Use the book for a short meditation and personal examination, as a self-guided retreat to call yourself to renewed dedication to Jesus' call, or for group discussion and renewed application of Jesus' teachings.

Books on the writings and spirituality of St. John of the Cross by Leonard Doohan:

The Contemporary Challenge of John of the Cross (1995)

John of the Cross: Your Spiritual Guide (2013)

The Dark Night is Our Only Light: A Study of the Book of the *Dark Night* by John of the Cross (2013)

John of the Cross—The Spiritual Canticle: The Encounter of Two Lovers. An Introduction to the Book of the *Spiritual Canticle* by John of the Cross (2013)

John of the Cross: *The Living Flame of Love* (2014)

A Year with St. John of the Cross: 365 Daily Readings and Reflections (2015)

See also, The Contemporary Challenge of St. Teresa of Avila (2016)

All books are available from amazon.com

Visit the author's webpage at *leonarddoohan.com*

Made in the USA
San Bernardino, CA
23 October 2018